Will The Real Me
Please Stand Up

by

Christopher Knopf

Will the Real Me Please Stand Up
© 2010 Christopher Knopf All rights reserved.

Published in the USA by:
BearManor Media
P O Box 71426
Albany, Georgia 31708
www.bearmanormedia.com

ISBN 1-59393-525-0

Printed in the United States of America.

Book design and layout by Darlene Swanson • www.van-garde.com

Dedication

Dedicated to my wife, Lorraine,
without whom I don't take his train.

With special thanks to John Gay and Wendy Cooper

Acknowledgments

To Dr. Jay Schapira, who kept me around long enough to write this book.

To David Felser, who threatened me with banishment if I didn't write it.

To David Rintels, for setting a very high bar.

To the Writers Guild of America, and all the writers over the years who've fought for all we've won.

To David Menefee, whose tireless and thorough editing helped me trough the narrows.

To Ben Ohmart, for saying yes.

Introduction

In 1974 when Lorraine and I decided to get married, she called her mother in Orlando, whom I'd yet to meet, to give her the news.

Her mother was delighted and responsive, asked, "What does he do?"

"He's a writer."

There was lingering silence on the other end of the line, finally broken by, "I meant for a living."

Forword

There's an old wheeze in Hollywood about the five stages of an actor's career. It applies to writers as well. It goes like this. Stage One, "Who's Chris Knopf?" Stage Two, "Get me Chris Knopf!" Stage Three, "Get me a Chris Knopf type." Stage Four, "Get me a young Chris Knopf." Stage Five, "Who's Chris Knopf?"

I know of very few writers in this business who ever beat it. "There are fewer stars for screen writers on the Hollywood Walk of Fame than there are for animals," Aljean Harmetz once wrote. And of those few that do have stars, only a few are etched in memory. Rod Serling, perhaps. Gene Roddenberry.

With luck and grit, after having been handed a very fortunate start and guessing right about a few open doors, I had the best of it for almost fifty years, nearly forty of which occupied Stage Two. It could be done in those days, starting out in the 1950s. There was work aplenty and opportunity to learn one's craft on the job, having waited your turn to move into and along with the stream of things. A fifty-year career was unusual, but thirty was not.

Today it's different. A writer, given youth and talent, can move into well-paying assignments years before most of us could or did. His or her tenure in this business today, however, is a short, ten years or so, unless breaking out with a blockbuster script or moving into a supervisorial position, too often replaced by writers no better than they, just younger. Such is the belief of those in power that youth must be served, and that only the youthful can do it. Are they right? It doesn't matter. They control the purse, and God help these young if they err. Spare them the death knell condemnation as early as their late-thirties with the all too common writer's epitaph, "He's lost it."

So given that this is a business that eats its young and discards its seasoned, how did I do it? I'll tell you how. I don't know. More important, why did I do it? Why choose to endure the insecurities, failures, lean economic years and sometimes devastating criticisms that inevitably come with writing. And having started in it, stumbling badly at the outset, why did I stay with it?

As such this is not a textbook on how to write or succeed in Hollywood. It is the story of one writer's journey, bucking heads with his own self-image to find out who he was. There were friends and obstacles, heroes and villains, people who helped, others who stuck their Gucci loafers out to trip anyone in their way. There was also the one to whom I was to become a reflection of himself, disappointed when I couldn't achieve it, unable to handle it when I did. There was also the bizarre. With a glass raised to one of the most memorable, let the journey begin.

Prologue

Just east of Beverly Hills, on the north side of Santa Monica Boulevard, was a tailor shop. I say was. Whether it's still there today, I've no idea, but during the fifties and sixties it was a Mecca for screen and television writers.

The tailor was Manny Dwork, and Manny loved writers, so much so the entire second floor of his two-story fading yellow stucco building was a warren of offices reserved exclusively for writers of screen and television for rentals hard to find anywhere else in town.

Writers came and went, sometimes for months, sometimes for years, yet forever returning, it seemed, some renowned, others not, but all sharing a bond and collegiality. There were Oscar nominees, Emmy winners, and, of course, there was Phyllis.

Phyllis was a mannequin, rescued from the trash bin behind Manny's building. If anything kept you on your toes it was Phyllis. Go into the bathroom, there she was on the toilet. Open the door to the stairway leading up, down she came, cascading toward you. Enter your office in the morning, there she'd be, feet sticking out from under the desk.

There was also three-time Academy Award nominated writer Walter Newman. Walter was my guru, and there he stood in my office door telling me of an assignment he couldn't take, but was mine if I wanted; he'd sold me to the producer. Robert Mitchum playing a simple man who comes to unwanted prominence in the Irish rebellion.

Mitchum, at this time in the early 1960s, was about as hot as Hollywood offered, shooting one film, a Western, with two more in the can awaiting release. Did I want to write a screenplay for him? After thirteen years of B and C movies, and some admittedly decent television, I would now be elevated into the rarefied realm of Chayefsky, Trumbo, Wilder and Brackett. This was it! My time had come!

I hurriedly broke down the story and met the producer, Raymond Stross, for dinner that night. Stross was every cliché Budd Schulberg ever imagined. An Englishman, there were the gaudy clothes, Cuban cigar, the beautiful hooker at the table. C------ F------'s hooker he proudly told me. There was also the hugely seductive smile, and the enthusiastic bobbing head and "Yes! Yes!" to everything I told him I wanted to do. Except he wasn't listening, and he was sweating.

Some things in life are pretty clear signs. Like a temperature of a 103°. Or Raymond Stross sweating. Sadly, I was only thirty something, and still pretty green, unaware of the signs. So I met him, as agreed, on Mitchum's set at MGM the following day as the morning shooting wrapped for lunch. Mitchum, in levis, hog leg and Stetson, lunged toward us, and past us, plowed into his trailer, slamming the door in our faces.

Stross beamed, "Isn't he capital?" and disappeared inside with Mitchum, and just as quickly came out again. Came out doesn't quite capture it; was ejaculated seems more the word.

"Eight o'clock tonight at Mitchum's office," he told me, still that grin.

Mitchum's office was on the Sunset Strip. Outside it was a hall. There I sat listening to angry voices inside. At nine o'clock the door flew open and Tay Garnet, one very prominent, red-faced director, stormed past me and out. I was beginning to get a message. But what?

At ten o'clock Stross stuck his beaming, sweating face out and summoned me inside.

A half-dozen people were in the room. There was Stross, and Riva, Mitchum's statuesque executive secretary who this night had one responsibility, keeping Mitchum's glass filled. There were the three obligatory suits from the William Morris Agency, led by the respected Phil Kellog, all looking like they'd rather be anywhere else.

Center room, in his power chair, sat Mitchum. He hadn't changed from the set, was still in costume, slouched on the small of his back, legs stretched out before him, Stetson slanted down completely hiding his face, drink hanging down at his side.

He made no move to look up when I entered, nor when I was introduced, even though Phil, whom I knew, greeted me warmly. Stross got to matters quickly. "Tell him, Christophuh, what brilliance you're bringing to the table."

There are times in life when you strike a blow for manhood.

"I'd like to know," I said, with a charge of testosterone, "what the hell's going on in here?"

The two suits' necks disappeared into their collars. Phil got involved with a sudden hangnail. Stross' eyeballs spun like pinwheels. Mitchum's head came up slowly and I saw his eyes. They were gazing at me as though I were fermenting yeast.

"I'll tell you what's going on," he said.

He was in a bar, in London, minding his own, when this little c--- s----- Stross came up to him, buying him drinks and flapping about some goddamn f------ project he had about the f------ IRA and he kept telling Stross, "No!" Except when he woke the next morning with a head from Chelsea to Frankfurt he found his f----- signature on some f------ contract this little s--- had shoved under his nose sometime during the night. He had no goddamn interest in doing it. He hated it. He was legally stuck with it. "Now what's your f------ idea?"

For thirty minutes I pitched to Mitchum, face hidden behind his hat again, Stross beaming encouragement, conducting, literally, to bring in the violins, mute the brass, crescendo to the finish as the suits nodded hopeful approval. When I was through there was silence.

"Well, what do you think?" I asked.

"I think," Mitchum answered, head rising to the suits, "we get another writer."

He was right. Talking to a faceless presence, I'd been awful though not for just that reason. So enamored was I with the prospect of the assignment I'd jumped in far too quickly, unprepared. Still there was a face to save, my own, if I could.

"Okay, what would you do?" I challenged.

"I'll tell you what I'd do," he said.

And he did.

"Absolutely brilliant!" Stross said when Mitchum was done. "A new writer. Yes! Yes!"

For once Stross got it right. Brilliant Mitchum was. I was floored. God could he tell a story. Creative, sensitive, witty.

A year later I read that Mitchum, while shooting the film in Ireland, got decked in a pub by a Paddy O' who'd had a pint too many. I liked hearing that, but biting good writer's nails I'm forced to admit, I liked the meeting more. The man was not a star for nothing, although I was later told I was out the door at "I'd like to know what the hell's going on?" Lesson learned, as others had been before, still others that would come later. As in all things there was a beginning.

Meat Shrinkage

My first job, as it was for many of us, was pumping gas. At least I thought that's what I was doing. I was two and a half years old.

We were living on the lower stretches of Tower Road in Beverly Hills. My father, Edwin Knopf, was engaged in a dual capacity at Paramount studios. It was 1930. Talkies were coming into vogue and one of his jobs, given his east coast theatrical background, acting, and owning his own theater in Baltimore, was to teach actors of the silent screen how to speak for "talkies." It was an assignment that drove him to two double scotches every night, an acquired taste that would stay with him the rest of his life.

The second was more rewarding, directing, mostly a series of programmers, now and then starring such as Jean Arthur and Fay Wray of *King Kong* fame.

It was a Sunday. My father had just purchased a brand new Packard that he liked to drive west on Wilshire Blvd, past the bean fields of Westwood to Sepulveda, turn south, and open her up to see if it would actually hit 80 as the salesman had assured him it could.

There the car rested in the driveway in all its virgin glory, and doing the best for Dad I thought I could do, decided to fill up her gas tank. Which I did. With the garden hose. The chastising I got from my father was one of two that linger to this day. The second was quite different. A letter.

1947. I'd graduated from high school in June a year and a half before, entered UCLA in September a month after the end of the war, turned eighteen on December 20th and the following day was notified to present myself at the local draft board. There I was given an option. Enlist now before the end of the term for a hard and fast eighteen months, or be drafted when the term was over. No guarantee of duration.

I enlisted. Then and there, that day. Four weeks to go in the school term. What inspired that choice had nothing to do with duration of time in the service, nor patriotism. Having gone to an all boys prep school in the hills just south of Santa Barbara, isolated from anything other than books and yearly lectures on sex (don't push girls into swimming pools when they don't want to go in), I entered UCLA and instantly majored in coeds, parties, and going to Bruin football games. If I had waited for my grades till the end of the term I'd have flunked half my courses. As it was, they generously gave me half credit for each course, with a grade C.

Still it wasn't a total loss. You could choose your branch of service at that time if you enlisted. I chose the Air Corps as it was known in those days, planes having always been my first love, and applied for flight school. Any kind of school willing to accept a teenage kid for anything short of officers training. Waist gunner, tail gunner, wing walker. I didn't care, just flight.

"Sorry," I was told, "flight schools are being shut down."

I applied to cryptography school, mathematics being my most accomplished subject in school.

"Sorry, war's over," I heard. "Nothing left to encrypt.'

So it was in the spring of 1947, nineteen years old, I found myself at the Army Air Corps Air Transport Command Base in Great

Falls, Montana, assigned to the Finance Department as a clerk typist. Base commander was an eagle Colonel, a big, beefy drunk, who rarely turned up except to qualify for his flight pay. One day, reportedly bombed out of his gourd, he cracked up a P-38 on take off, surviving the event as most drunks do. The plane didn't.

There was only one thing in the Air Corps at the time that you could write off as a financial loss: meat shrinkage. Purchase a thousand pounds of beef from Kansas City, by the time it got to your base it weighed 990 pounds. Write off ten pounds. That one loophole became a catchall, mostly for officers, writing off a lost flight jacket or cap. Everybody understood the game and it was accepted until our base commander decided to write off a $350,000 P-38 to meat shrinkage. The subsequent military investigation of the base and its operations were made public, finding their way into a national magazine.

Base headquarters was a network of offices, a barber shop, and one immense hangar, located just off the airstrip, a half mile from our tar paper barracks, mess hall and outside latrines. Winter nights, twenty-seven degrees below zero, latrines were ignored for the coal burning stoves center room in our sleeping quarters. Recreation was limited. In the Finance Department we were inventive. On the first of every month was a football game. Like clock work under armed guard, early morning on every first, a canvas sack was delivered to our office, a quarter of a million dollars in cash, the monthly base payroll. That was our football.

The finance department also had an outstanding basketball team, walking off with the championship in league play largely due to Johnston and Shivers, both of whom would later play college ball. We decimated everyone, especially the officers. In a game we won 92-8, playing guard, I dove for a loose ball along with the base adjutant, a lieutenant colonel. I got to it first. He got to my neck with a hammer lock. Infuriated, I slammed my elbow into his face, followed with a roundhouse to his stomach, the air exploding from his lungs...

Don't I wish. As I lay there, suffocating, I offered appropriate military protocol. "Sorry, sir. No excuse, sir."

With all of it, I loved my time in the Air Corps. The war being over, things were relaxed. Friendships quickly evolved, fellow recruits I never would have met anywhere else. There were farm kids from the Midwest, a cowboy from Texas, street kids from Cleveland, and of course the hero to us all, Private Bonelli. A thirty-five year old lifer, three times busted from sergeant, he taught us how to slide a dice instead of rolling it, so you'd never come up with craps.

For me there was something else. During each sparingly given fifteen-minute break from checking and rechecking payroll payments, I could be found in that hangar. All my life I'd been fascinated by planes, built models of them, gas powered, rubber band powered, gliders and there in that hangar were the real things. A World War II P-51. An AT-6 advanced trainer. I was in the Air Corps, it said so on my shoulder patch, and never once had I gotten off the ground. Until one day.

"Want to go up?"

He was standing, one arm leaning on the wing of the AT-6. His name was Captain Schmidt. I'd seen him around, a grizzled veteran of the war, worn cap that looked like a tank had rolled over it, soiled jacket.

"Get a parachute."

Stuffed into the rear seat of an ancient L-5 spotter plane, I watched us lumber down the runway, lift off at sixty knots. The first thing that hit me was parachute or not, there was no way out, made all the more apparent as we flew into the mountains. Never more than 500 feet above ground, Schmidt, no warning, threw the plane into spins and snap rolls, cursing that he wasn't getting it right.

Thirty minutes out it happened. Hop scotching over and through canyons and crevasses, peaks all around us, three hundred feet over the ground now, the motor stopped. Stopped! Schmidt was pointing vigorously down, down at a clearing just ahead of us. *Jesus! A forced, crash landing! My first time ever in a plane and I'm going to die!*

When I saw it. Ahead in that clearing was a grizzly. Schmidt had feathered the prop, was gliding in behind it. Fifty yards from it he hit the throttle. The engine sprang to life. So did the grizzly, and beat us, literally, across the meadow and into the woods as Schmidt, roaring in delight, pulled the plane up over the trees.

When we got back I wrote my parents about the experience, a four-page detailed letter.

My father answered as fast as the mail allowed. "Two things," he wrote, and I could sense his hyperventilation. "First, don't you ever, ever again, not *ever* write a letter like that to your mother! You scared her half to death! And second, you just might be a writer."

My God! He Made His Hand Disappear!

A Writer? Me? Never. Not in the cards. I didn't have anything to write about. Besides, spelling was not my strong suit. Aviation was my future.

Taking no furloughs while in the service, I was discharged a month and a half early in the summer of 1947, my unused furlough pay tacked onto my discharge. Returning home to Santa Monica where we now lived, I promptly spent every dime on flying lessons at the local airport, reentered UCLA on the GI Bill, and resumed my mathematic and scientific march toward becoming what I'd always dreamed of becoming, an aeronautical engineer.

But it meant something else. It meant living at home again for the first time in six years, having been away four at boarding school, then nearly two in the military, and therein lay the problem. For reasons clearer later than then, my father and I did not get along.

At the time, even earlier, as a child, my day began when I heard the start of his car, and ended when I heard it return. As a preteen, working weekend afternoon's in my room on a model plane while listening to a ball game, he would enter, a look of annoyed displeasure on his face, and tell me to work on the model or listen to the game, one or the other, it was impossible to do both. Always that, or some negative equivalent.

The house was two story, an elaborate circular stairway climbing to Dad's and my Mother's quarters in the front of the house, a narrow stairway leading to the children's in the rear. Between the two quarters was a hallway, separated one from the other by a door with a high unreachable lock. We were forbidden to use the front stairs. Still, I often waited till no one was home, sneaked up the front stairs into Dad's room, went through his closet, his bath room, opened drawers, trying to unravel the mystery of who he was.

Mother was different. Doing all she could to compensate, she allowed us into her room, which was separate from Dad's, would come to kiss us good night as she and Dad were heading out to a party or restaurant when we'd inevitably hear Dad's bellow from below, "Mildred! Leave those children alone!"

Yet there were times. A bunch of us, then sixth and seventh graders, decided to take our touch football game down to the fifteenth fairway on the Riviera Country Club Golf course below our street. Chased off, we scampered back up the embankment, only to encounter a waiting squad car, Cop and Groundskeeper.

"What'll we do with 'em?" the Cop asked with a fearful frown. "Take 'em down and throw the key away?"

Giving up our names and phone numbers, we headed home. Terrified what Dad would say, I found him jovial, thinking the whole thing was a kick, wanting to know who'd won the game, how I'd played. Further, no stone was left unturned when it came to education. Piano lessons were provided. So were French lessons, and tennis lessons. There were theater and concerts. His support of whatever choices I chose to make for myself, however, was rare. Later, much later, I would sense why, but not then.

Born into a well-known New York German Jewish family, Dad,

"Eddie" as he was known to his friends, an extraordinarily handsome youth and man, found himself handicapped by two events beyond his control. The first was his brother, Alfred, born seven years earlier, who was, by aged twenty-two on his way to becoming America's most prestigious literary publisher. The second took place in Germany shortly after World War I.

In an event often told, Dad was with friends in a night club in Bavaria, having come there for the early spring skiing. A fortune teller was making the rounds. Coming to Dad, she took his hand, gravely announced he was to be extremely cautious the following day, warning of an accident if he was not.

The next morning as they gathered to take on the mountain, Dad announced, "Look. I'm not superstitious, but it's on my mind. I'll probably fall and break a leg. I'm not going."

Staying behind with a friend who remained to keep him company, the two ordered lunch at an outdoor café. While it was being prepared, they sauntered across the street to a wine shop. It was not an ordinary place of business. Wine bottles stood exposed on racks, but none were filled with wine. True to German ingenuity, some might say culture, the bottles had been filled with gunpowder left over from the Kaiser's war three years earlier. They were, in effect, home made hand grenades. That night, arming them by pulling their corks, volunteers, given five seconds, were to throw them at a huge erected mound of snow where they detonated in a sparkling shower of ice. As Dad and his friend admired the bottles on display, a young boy picked one up by the cork. The bottle fell free. Dad grabbed it, headed for the door where it exploded. The door got most of it, but Dad got the rest, a chest full of shrapnel, as well as the loss of his left hand.

Superficially Dad handled both well, especially the amputation. Happening at the age of twenty-two, immersed as he'd become in the New York theatrical scene, it brought him attention he'd never achieved under his brother's overpowering image. No woman could resist him, especially the beauteous Mary Ellis of the Metropolitan Opera. They married, the union quickly souring and ending in divorce. The maid of honor at that wedding? One Mildred Oppenheimer.

Knowing Dad since they were teenagers, she had always been in love with him, wanted only to take care of him, in fact turned down a marriage proposal from George Gershwin, marrying my father instead. It was a fifty-eight year marriage, during which she gave birth to three children.

I was the oldest child. When I was twelve, hearing about the Gershwin rejection, I'm told I said to her, "Mom! How could you have *done* that to me?"

Whatever furies chased my father through his life, the loss of his hand never outwardly appeared to be one of them. He never gave in to it, never allowed it to become a handicap. He became an excellent tennis player, ping pong player, and swimmer. He drove a stick shift car. He had dinner forks personally designed with a knife edge attached replacing one of the tines so he could easily cut his food. Shirts, tailor made, were cuffed about the stump of his left arm at the wrist. People could be in his company for an hour before gasping in realization the hand was missing. During the war he visited VA hospitals in the area, encouraging wounded veteran amputees. Yet as many a soldier who'd suffered what Dad had gone through, he was a victim of what we called then "shell shock," more euphemistically phrased today as "post traumatic syndrome," which translated, at unpredictable times, into bouts of excessive and irrational irritation and behavior.

Still, with it all, there were memorable moments. One night the violinist, Jasha Heifitz, whom mother had known since both were fifteen, came to dinner with his new wife, a first meeting for my parents. During dinner Dad performed one of his parlor tricks, placing a fork on the stump of his left arm, covering it with a napkin, whisking the napkin away, the fork disappearing. Heifitz' wife shrieked, "My God! He made his hand disappear!"

As for Alfred, Dad adored him. At least gave the impression he did. It was his father, my grandfather, Sam Knopf, that was the bête noir of Dad's existence. Sam, to whom Alfred was all things, the light of Sam's life. Dad? A footnote in Sam's resume, a disappointment compared to Alfred, who'd graduated from Columbia University at nineteen, with honors, captain of the track team, establishing his own publishing house three years thereafter.

The cost to Dad became known to me years later, after his death, when I discovered an unfinished autobiography he had started. In it was this:

"You have no right to sit at that table," he quoted his father, my grandfather as saying.

The "table" was the famous Round Table at the Algonquin. The year was 1920, Dad as old as the century.

"I've every right," my father answered.

"Based on what?"

"I've been invited."

"By whom?"

"Joe Hergesheimer."

"Opportunism. A friend of your brother's."

"Several times by Henry Mencken."

"Another friend of your brother's. For you to sit at that table puts you in the position of living on an intellectual income for which you do not have the capital. At best they will tolerate you. You will regret having been tolerated at the Round Table."

It was a ghost Dad fought all of his days. Not the least of which was to surround himself, as did Alfred, with the accomplished and famous who so famously flocked to Alfred, many of whom were handed off to my Father.

Artur Rubenstein, Heifitz, Gregor Piatagorsky, Jerome Kern, Richard Rogers, Oscar Hammerstein, Thomas Mann, F. Scott Fitzgerald, not to mention every prominent star, writer, director and producer in Hollywood. Clark Gable, Lana Turner, Irene Dunne, Louis B Mayer, Dinah Shore, Katherine Hepburn, Audrey Hepburn, Margaret Sullavan, George Cukor, Gregory Peck, Joan Fontaine, Spencer Tracy, Deborah Kerr, Frederic March, Fred Astaire, Angela Lansbury, Ronald and Nancy Reagan. Nearly everybody who was anybody in film or the arts or theater or the classical musical world could be found on any given Saturday night at our home on La Mesa Drive in Santa Monica, some wag churlishly claiming, "Living under Eddie and Mildred Knopf is waiting for the next name to drop."

Among the most memorable was Screen writer Herman Mankiewicz who'd pop two sleeping pills into his mouth as he left for his home in Beverly Hills twenty minutes away, on the theory by the time he got there he'd be ready for bed.

Screen Writer Charlie Lederer was everyone's favorite, and inevitably the stuff of wit and legends. Married to Orson Welles' former wife, Virginia, they had a fight one night.

"I'm leaving," she announced.

"Go on! Go!" Charlie challenged.

"If I had any money..."

"No problem."

Writing her a check for a thousand dollars, he threw it at her. Driving to the Beverly Wilshire Hotel six blocks away, she put the check on deposit, got her room, washed her hair. There was a knock on the door. *Charlie*, she figured, enjoying a sense of victory, but opened the door to the hotel night manager.

"Mrs Lederer?"

"Yes."

"This check," he said, holding it out to her. "We can't accept it."

"What's wrong with it?"

"Read it."

It was made out to Virginia Lederer, for $1,000, signed Peter Rabbit. The story wasn't lost on me. I would later pay homage to it.

Dad, too, had his punch lines, loving to puncture pretense and prejudice. Like Charlie, he was brilliant at it. Invited to lunch at Los Angeles' California Club one day his host suggested Dad become a member.

"I can't become a member here," Dad answered.

"Why not?" his host inquired.

"They don't take Jews."

His host was disbelieving, got up to gain confirmation, returned red-faced and embarrassed.

"How did you know?" he asked.

"Because," Dad replied, "the food's so bad."

Not to be outdone, Mother had her own sly moments. At a gala charity evening, she found herself seated at the same table with Betty Hutton. The star was holding forth.

"He was absolutely one of the most f------ a—- h---- I ever worked with. He was just so full of s---. I mean, he was ridiculous."

Ah!" interjected Mother. "A synonym."

At their own house, however, my parents guests were always well and warmly served, Dad, by then, a well regarded contract producer at MGM, so outwardly elegant, charming, sophisticated.

Mother, in her own right, was extraordinary. A playwright in her early years, multilingual, she was able to converse in five languages. She'd been a pianist, artist, and an incredible botanist with a garden of over a hundred rose bushes, most of them different, one from the other, all of which she personally tended. She had headed the Voluntary Army Canteen Service at nearby Fort MacArthur in the early forties during the war, was now the remarkable endearing hostess, brilliant in the kitchen, who was in the midst of writing her second of seven published cook books. What my father sought, mother attracted.

There was Rubenstein often at the piano when he wasn't holding court, trying his hand at boogie-woogie. "Whenever I play it," he said one night, "it sounds like bad Bach." Piatagorsky and Heifitz playing string quartets accompanied by renowned musicians brought in from the Los Angeles Philharmonic, equally accompanied by food, conversation and wine.

There, first as children, later as teens, I and my younger sister, Wendy, and my much younger brother, Jonathan, would be called downstairs to be paraded before the guests till dinner was called.

I was never comfortable with this ritual, always feeling painfully inadequate, overwhelmed, which left me unsure how to relate. Did I talk to these people? How? What did I have to say? My sister seemed better at it than I, while Jonathan had his own little game. He'd go along till the room was cleared for dinner, than empty all the remaining drinks into one glass and down it.

It was 1948 now. I was twenty. Following a full year at UCLA, along with that previous half term before going into the Air Corps and with just concluded summer school, I was about to enter the fall semester as a junior. I was doing well in college, the break in the military maturing me. I was not doing well at home. The tension between Dad and me was growing by the day. Whether Dad was acting out with me what his father had acted out with him, who knows? Mostly it was a battle for control, Dad's over me, mine over myself. It all came to a head one Saturday evening just before fall registration.

Never having gone to college, Dad, despite his own father's assessment of him, had become incredibly self-educated in the arts, conversation, politics, language, literature. Along that line he had a magnificent collection, possibly every significant classical musical piece ever recorded on the old seventy-eights. We were in the den where his collection stood in a huge made-to-order floor-to-ceiling mahogany case. He pulled out a Brahms, set it on the turn table and turned to me. I was seated on one of two facing couches separated by a coffee table before the fire place.

Dad pointed to an arm chair mid-room. "Sit there," he told me.

"Why?" I asked.

"You can't get the full value of the music where you are. Sit there."

"I'm fine," I told him.

"That's not the place to hear this music! That chair is!"

"I'm fine."

"Are you going to do what I tell you or not?" Dad asked.

"I'm fine," I repeated.

"Fine!" he responded, yanking the needle off the record, scratching it as he did so. The scratching ripped it, made him furious. Words were exchanged and for the first time in my life my feelings spilled over and I stood toe to toe with my father. It wouldn't be the last. Years later when my mother was in the hospital and I'd moved in to watch over Dad at night, giving way to daytime nurses arriving to look after him till I could return in the evening, we had the ultimate blow out. Preparing to leave for work at Fox I entered to find him firing the nurses, which effectively prevented me from going anywhere. I told the nurses they were to stay. Dad blew.

"This is *my* house!" he hollered.

"No," I answered. "This is *my* house as long as I'm here!"

"Don't you talk to *me*!"

"Dad?"

"Not ever!"

The heat rose up and boiled over.

"You are the most selfish human being I've ever known in my life!" I told him.

"Well, you're a son of a bitch!"

"If I'm a son of as bitch," I countered, "guess what that makes you?"

He stared at me as though I'd hit him. "You and I've got as lot of unfinished business," he said.

"You bet we do."

That would be decades later. As I stood there in his den that day, twenty years-old, matching his rage with mine, his hand fluttered to his chest.

"You're going to give me a heart attack! I'm going to have a heart attack!"

Panicked, I bolted from the room, got into my car and drove north into the night. I got as far as Ventura, sixty miles away, turned around and limped home.

The following morning we confronted each other. He was at breakfast. Without looking up from his paper he apologized for the "heart attack" line.

"You know the problem?" I braved. "You won't let me go."

"No," he answered. "You haven't got the guts to go."

That day I took off for Berkeley 400 miles north, signed appropriate transfer papers, and registered at the University of California. It was a turning point in my life.

One Long, Three Short

The campus of U.C. Berkeley, across the bay from San Francisco, with its signature campanile, was at that time in the fall of 1948, home to approximately 20,000 students, many of whom were veterans returned from World War II. Some married, some with children, the opportunity provided them through the GI Bill was immense: tuition, books, up to $250 a month for living expenses. To the majority of them, most in their mid-to-late twenties, this was their shot. And they made the most of it. The competition was insane, the University getting it into their heads to grade on the curve. The best got "A" grades, the second best "B's," and so on. Academically it was a nightmare challenge, and the most rewarding I'd faced.

The faculty was renowned. Several, all scientists were Nobel Laureates, seldom seen, sequestered as they were in the cyclotron up Strawberry Canyon above campus with their handful of selected graduate students. Several more were among the twenty nation-wide academicians called upon by Congress to write the history of the war just ended. Among them were John Hicks and Raymond Sontag, Hicks liberal, Sontag conservative, from whom I took Hicks' History of the U.S., Sontag's History of Europe, both classes covering 1900 to the then present day.

For living quarters I applied to and was accepted into International House, "I House" as it was called, rooming with a so called "White Russian" who'd escaped to the west through Siberia. One of four in the world, (Universities of Chicago, Columbia, and the Sorbonne being the others), the eight-story I House was made up of 500 students, half foreign, half American. The friendships I made there, many of them, would last through much of our lives. Sadly, at this writing, I've survived all but one. Among them was Zulfikar Ali Bhutto, later to become Premier of Pakistan, who was executed in 1979 following a military coup, his daughter Benazir Bhutto, trying to follow in his footsteps, recently slain by an assassin.

We worked hard during the week, played hard on weekends, battling each other in canoes on the Russian River, into the Sierras for skiing, touch football, both men and women, in the parks above campus. When the 1950 Egyptian-Israeli war broke out, Mohammed Mortada, an Egyptian friend and I heard about it on my car radio as we headed into the Sierra foothills for a weekend of fishing. We solved the whole problem in two hours.

Berkeley being Berkeley, there was the usual foment. Mario Savio would later have his day over free speech. Ours was the loyalty oath.

It was pre-McCarthy, but the fear of Communism was running rampant throughout the country. Especially on campuses. University professors, intellectual, liberal for the most part, were looked upon with suspicion, much of the public convinced they were indoctrinating its unwashed youth in the ways of Marx and Lenin. The Board of Regents of the University acted in late 1949. All faculty members would have to sign an oath pledging loyalty to the United States by June the following year, or be fired.

2,000 professors, the University's entire Academic Senate, responded with rage, and in that they were supported by virtually the entire student body. First, as employees of the University, a state institution, they were employees of the State of California. As such they had signed such an oath as a condition of employment, ordered to do so, as were all state employees, by the state's duly elected governing body. Second, and most importantly, this new, and duplicating edict came from a body *appointed* by the Governor, none *elected*, and therefore, in the academics' view, supported by the overwhelming student body, without constitutional authority to demand such a thing.

There were protest meetings, both professors and students, and marches through the streets of Berkeley. There were no bon fires, flag burnings or disruptions of classes as would later happen in the 1960s, but there was profound anger nonetheless. An immense gathering took place in the University amphitheater, at which the Regents promised to come and give their side. No Regents showed, inflaming the crowd and culminating in a historic declaration. To a man and woman the academic senate declared no one, not one of them, would ever sign such an oath!

June came. Thirty-one of the 2,000 held firm. Just thirty-one. All the rest signed the oath. Sadly I recall the professor of my Romantic Poetry class, who swore he'd never succumb to such an edict, was among those that did.

"I believe I owe you all an explanation," he said addressing the class. "We, as educators, have only one weapon with which to fight, and that's reason. If our opponents refuse to meet us on that battlefield, we are powerless. Further," he concluded, his face filling with sadness, "it is my belief that academics, by and large, are timid people."

It was still a great class. Wordsworth, Byron, Shelley, Blake and Keats were well served.

As for those that were fired, Professor Musactine of my Chaucer class among them, the thirty-one found their way to no less than Harvard, Princeton, Brown and Yale, later suing the University for wrongful dismissal. It was a suit they won, their leaving all but gutting the English and Political Science Departments. It would be a decade before these departments returned to prominence.

Amazingly, through it all, school went on. Most curiously, however, I'd lost my appetite for mathematics. I'd never been that much of a reader, and now suddenly I was. I switched to English as a major, deciding upon a career in teaching for lack of knowing what else to do with myself. Then one day it happened.

I had earlier taken a short story literature class from Mark Schorer, a well-known writer for *The New Yorker* on staff at Cal. I'd written a paper on Irwin Shaw's *The Eighty Yard Run*. The note I got back read, "As usual your writing captivates and moves the reader. Regrettably, as usual, you have marred the essay with spelling errors, which forces me to lower an 'A' grade to a 'B' for the paper."

Captivates? Moves? I had written a long, humorous poem for the school's newspaper, the *Daily Californian*, but that was it. On a whim I applied to Schorer's short story writing class the following spring term. Thirteen out of forty applicants were to be accepted. To cover my bet I also applied to novelist George Stewart's novel writing course, samples of writing submitted to each for qualification.

I got accepted to both, but could not take both. I had no thoughts for a short story, but did for a novella. Though the idea of ever putting it to paper had never entered my mind.

Late summer 1948, following summer school at UCLA, just before transferring to Berkeley, I joined my father in London where he was making a film for MGM. After a brief tour through France, we headed home on the Queen Mary. As the great ship steamed up the Hudson toward its west side Manhattan dock, I noticed the several tugs working it into its berth were taking commands from a series of varying blasts from the liner's horn: two long, one short; or one long, three short. Each were instructions to the tug captains of what was called for to negotiate the huge ship into its berth. *What, I mused, if one of the tugs screwed up and got it wrong?*

The idea percolated and came to fruition in Professor Stewart's class. A tug captain, with a crew of three, his tug as well as himself not long from the junkyard, has spent his life working banana boats and rust buckets from Honduras, forever envious of those assigned to the arrivals of the great liners, convinced only the fates have conspired to keep him from achieving his dream. Through a shortage of tugs one day, he gets his treasured assignment to join the tugs on the Queen. Totally stepping out of character he becomes a martinet, screws up the assignment, sends the liner crashing into her dock.

Whether my father was the captain of that tug, and I the first mate desperately trying to head off disaster, I've never pieced together. But the novella, written in college, staying in college, was sent to my father, who sent it on to Dore Schary, second in command to Louis B Mayer at the time at MGM. I was told to report to Metro following graduation. A position awaited me as a Junior Writer at $75 a week. I took an apartment in Westwood and reported to work.

Cut the Cackle and
Get to the Burn

I would like to say that recognition of a budding new talent got me to Metro. It didn't, as the studio's famous lion, Leo, smirking down from his perch high atop stage fifteen, seemed to know as I drove onto the MGM parking lot that first day. In truth, I and six other sons and nephews of MGM's elite were brought into the studio as "trainees", to keep us from loading bags at Safeway. Few, if any of us, had anything in our resumes to justify inviting us aboard. It was nepotism, pure and simple, not that rare in the industry then.

We were assigned to Academy Award-winning writer-producer Charlie Schnee. "Schnee White and the Seven Dwarfs" they dubbed us, "The Sons of the Pioneers." The fact that some of us would eventually achieve creditable careers was no tribute to anyone's foresight, nor should it have been.

Among the seven I was the one with aspirations of becoming a writer, but I never did see much of Charlie Schnee, who avoided the lot of us at all costs. Alone among the others I was grudgingly suffered at lunch at the Writers Table in the studio commissary as long as I didn't say much. For good reason. At any sitting were a dozen Academy Award winners or nominees, not to mention renowned authors and Broadway playwrights, the conversation crackling, witty.

It was more than daunting. "Advice, dear boy?" Leonard Spigelgass counseled me one day when I asked him for it. "I'll give it to you, the best you'll get. Texaco's hiring." Later, much later, when success and awards began to accumulate my way, Spigelgass proudly proclaimed, "And I was the first to give him encouragement."

Abandoned by Charlie Schnee, I was absorbed into my father's unit, given an office two down from his, told to read a massive pile of successful screenplays, find a story of my own and write, turning in pages weekly to Dad as I did so. Two things I must say: he knew the craft and he made me work. If I didn't finish twenty pages for the week, in I had to come on Saturday and Sunday to complete it.

"I've got friends to meet in Malibu this Sunday," I once protested.

"No, you've got a second act to meet in your office this Sunday," he answered.

His criticisms were brutal but accurate. I once described a room in a period piece I was writing as, "It's decorated in the period of the times."

"What's that mean?" he asked.

"Well, you know."

"I haven't a clue."

MGM had a magnificent art department and library. I immersed myself in both, defiantly wrote a full page description of that room.

"Better," Dad said. "Now do it in ten lines." When that was done, "Now do it in three." Lesson learned. And not the only one.

When I didn't develop the energizing event that should capture my reader until well into my script, he told me to read Shaw's introduction to *Saint Joan*.

"Why?"

"Read it."

There it was in Shaw's long winded review of the audience opening night of his play on Joan of Arc. A half hour in, a patron reportedly leapt to his feet, cupped his hands to his mouth and shouted, "Cut the cackle and get to the burn!"

Still, for me, FADE IN – EXT.

Nothing captivating or moving in that, or much else that followed. I was despairing, utterly overwhelmed, in the big leagues where I didn't belong, much less the minors. Then one day at the Writers Table Frances Goodrich couldn't open a bottle of ketchup.

At the end of the table sat writer-director Richard Brooks. Unshaven, crew cut, pipe clenched upside down in his teeth, he looked macho as hell. He called for the bottle. He couldn't open it.

Sitting next to him was Millard Kaufman. Millard had recently been brought aboard by Dore Schary, now studio head with Mayer's retirement, to write a screenplay about military training, for which Millard would soon receive his first of two Academy nominations, and which, ironically enough, Brooks was to direct. Millard opened it.

Brooks' face turned scarlet. An ex-Marine who liked to tell of walking into barracks announcing, "I'm a Jew, and if any of you bastards don't like it, step outside!" Brooks suggested they do just that and settle things. Maybe it's what Brooks saw in Millard's eyes, or the fact that Millard, also an ex-Marine, had been a platoon leader in the landing assaults on Guam and Okinawa while Brooks had never gotten west of Hawaii, or that Millard was, in 1936 certified as the strongest man ever to enter Johns Hopkins University.

Whatever his reasons, Brooks took the wiser course and quickly decided the whole thing was a joke.

Struck with admiration and envy, I returned to my office, reviewed what I'd been writing, and sank into a funk. *Texaco? They were really hiring?*

There was a knock on the door. It was Millard. I don't know what he'd seen or sensed, but he wanted to talk. What was I doing, how was it going, anything I'd like him to read? Maybe he saw in me one of those raw, uncertain recruits he'd once led into combat. Whatever, that was the start of it. Over the next months I learned more about writing from Millard, reading his screenplay, being invited by him to see the rough cut of his movie, than I thought I could learn in my life. "You're better than you think you are," he'd tell me. "Don't quit."

We're All Your Friends, If You Make It

"Ornately produced costumer of 17th century court intrigue involving England's King Charles" wrote Leonard Maltin in his 1996 Movie and Video Guide, giving it three stars out of five.

"It" was *The King's Thief*, my first produced screenplay, released in the early 1950's. I joined the Screen Writers Guild. My pay was raised to Guild minimum, $187.50 per week. I was signed by an agent, Ned Brown of MCA. The cast, for a first time writer, was impressive. David Niven, Ann Blyth, Roger Moore, George Sanders. My father produced, Robert Z. "Pop" Leonard directed. Despite Maltin's kind review four decades later, those at the time were brutal.

Looking back on it, they were right. There was a naïveté to the writing. I was only twenty-four when assigned to the project, partially due to my supposed knowledge of Restoration English history coming out of Berkeley. Oh, it had all the prerequisites, the chases, duels and intrigue, the sly confrontations, even a sense of language, but captivating and moving? It didn't happen. It was manufactured, cartoonish, and frankly plain corny.   Something else though, was dooming my tenure at Metro. Television had arrived, bringing serious inroads into motion picture sales. The major studios were hit, and hit hard, particularly MGM which, unlike Universal and Warner Brothers, stubbornly refused to move into the new entertainment form. Cost-cutting was called for. To measure where, Loews, Inc, owner of Metro, sent their chief accountant west from New York. The untouchables were the studio executives, top-heavy in number, one with the sole responsibility, according to Charlie Lederer, of warning of glaciers should they suddenly appear over the Santa Monica Mountains. You could set your watch, it was rumored at the Writers table, by the flood of execs leaving the Thalberg Building at one o'clock each day on their way to the races at Hollywood Park.

True to most corporate downsizing, the heads of the studio, as advised, cut from the bottom. Writers were no longer to have their own secretaries. A pool, made up of half the secretaries previously on payroll, was set up to type writers' scripts. The effect of that cost cutting measure? Highly paid writers, all the while on salary under week to week contracts, found themselves sitting around playing gin rummy, waiting days to get their scripts typed due to understaffing and backlogs.

As for me, it was Herbie Baker's last day, too. As I drove behind him on my way out of the parking lot, he was stopped by a studio guard. Herbie, a comedy writer and brilliant comic lyricist, had just completed an assignment for Metro. Could he please open the back of his car trunk, the guard asked. Nothing personal, just studio policy for those leaving the lot. Grousing, Herbie did as told and almost had a heart attack. Inside were a half dozen typewriters, the guard, of course, in on the gag. Charlie Lederer, as always, was the usual suspect.

As I drove off the lot I couldn't help a backward glance at Leo, encircled high above in his famous MGM logo, "Ars Gratia Artis".

"Just remember we're all your friends," he seemed to be saying, tauntingly adding, "if you make it."

Kid, I'm Gonna Screw Somebody... It's Gonna Be A Bank

I'd met Bette McKeehan at MGM. At twenty-two, bright, committed, she was an executive secretary in the Metro story department, not an easy position to hold for one that young. Her parents liked me, my parents liked her, which possibly proved to be an energizing factor. We were married in 1951, both just twenty-three, neither of us sure exactly who we were, certainly not I.

Four years later, with two children and a third on the way, we were living in a small 1,300-square-foot home near Los Angeles Airport. I was out of work with no prospects. Nobody was falling in line to hire me. The favored comment when my agency called a prospective employer was, "He's Eddie Knopf's son, how good can he be?"

Then one day I got a call from Ned Brown, head of the writers' department at MCA. Though he'd signed me to the agency, I'd been immediately turned over to junior agents, eager and willing, but as new at the game as I. Be in his office at nine the following morning, I was told. If Ned wanted to see me personally something momentous had to be brewing. I wasn't wrong.

MCA was located in a baronial two-story building on the eastern flank of Beverly Hills, prime real estate. Dressed in coat and tie, I was ushered directly into Ned's office. He sat on a sort of elevated throne, as I recall, and handed me a piece of paper without comment.

"What is it?" I asked.

"Your release," he told me.

That was that. MCA, the largest, most powerful agency in town, had interest only in representing writers who, unless major players, were under studio contract and therefore steadily employed. They were not in the business of career building. Not for neophyte writers, and neither, I quickly discovered, was anyone else.

For the next two months, heart in my throat, I trudged from one agency to another, wasting hours in reception rooms, hoping for meetings that didn't occur. I had never gone through sleepless nights before, but then I did. I was scared, and so was Bette. Our two children, infants though they were, were subjected to shouting matches, slamming doors, and deadly silences. Looking back on it, there was no blaming Bette. She had quit her secure, highly responsible job at MGM to care for the kids, and now a third was soon to be due. We had just purchased a house in Westchester for the outrageous sum of $17,400, and how were we going to make the payments? I had never gone to my father for money. I wouldn't. I just plain couldn't. I'd always felt I somehow hadn't lived up to his expectations, and dreaded that this would validate his assessment. There was no going to banks. We had no collateral.

Then the doubts.

Did I really, after all, truly want to be a writer? Despite Millard Kaufman's encouragement was I really cut out to be one? Or was it something I'd been dragged into, exposed my first time out.

I'd like to say I'd caught the bug. That I'd been infected at the Metro writers table by all those incredible talents. I hadn't. Awed by them, yes, but I had no thoughts I could ever enter their company. So where was I? There was nothing else I knew how to do, nothing else I'd been prepared for.

I ran a blank page into my typewriter, and stared and stared.

Write something, dammit, write!

Somewhere inside me I sensed there were things I wanted to say, a hair ball defying me to cough it up, *but what? Anyway, what did it matter? I wasn't going anywhere to voice it, and besides, who'd care to hear it even if I knew what it was?*

The Gods intervened in the form of Sam Adams. A young agent with the Ingo Preminger Agency, Sam was unpretentious, non-establishment, drove a Volkswagen, loved chamber music. Years later, when he came to me to recommend a writer he represented whom he thought would be good for a series I'd developed and was producing, Adams was not interested in going through a laundry list of other writers he represented when I asked who else he had in his fold. That was the one he came to talk about, nobody else. His confidence was infectious. I hired the writer. Maybe that's what Adams did for me thirteen years earlier. Signing me with the Preminger agency, he found me a job at Columbia Studios.

Charles Schneer (not to be confused with Schnee) had purchased a story for a motion picture eventually released under the title *Twenty Million Miles To Earth*. Schneer, master of the low budget myth and fantasy programmer, needed a writer, a cheap one, me, working week to week at Writers Guild minimum, as long as I promised to deliver it fast. I got the assignment, turning up each day after a two hour cross town ride on multiple buses, Bette and the kids having need of our one car.

It was a monster picture. When it was released in 1957, reviews were surprisingly generous, the picture becoming a sort of cult classic due to the incredible stop-motion miniature work of Ray Harryhausen. Working at Columbia, however, was intimidating. First, a functionary from the story department would come calling each Friday.

"How many pages are you turning in this week?" he'd ask.

"I'm on page thirty," I'd say.

"You were on page thirty last week."

"I've been rewriting the first thirty pages."

"So you're turning in nothing this week, is that right?"

"No, I'm turning in thirty rewritten pages."

"In other words, nothing."

Further, if I stepped out onto the street to circle the building thinking through a scene, I was clocked out as leaving the studio during working hours. As for the offices, most were windowless, giving one the sense of solitary confinement. There was no commissary, only a rooftop area where I could take a home-packed lunch, unless venturing out to one of the coffee shops close by, clocked out as I left.

It all came down from Harry Cohn, head of the studio.

Considered a tyrant, he had a private dining room, at which a few select writers, producers and director were privileged to attend for lunch. Never a part of it, I was told you got to the room early to avoid being the last one in, blanching at the prospect of having to sit beside the glowering mogul. Considered irascible, arrogant, mean spirited, the fact remains Harry Cohn had his stamp on some of the most engaging, memorable movies of all time, with sensitive incisive themes that totally contradicted his reputation.

Indirectly, Cohn was also responsible for my remaining at Co-

lumbia for my next assignment. Finishing the script for Schneer, I
was awaiting notice to vacate my office, when a call came from Lillian
Burns. I had first met Lillian at Metro where she'd been in charge of
new acting talent signed by the studio. By then, she was Cohn's chief
lieutenant, tough, no nonsense, as feared as he. Meeting Lillian in
her office, I was told there was an assignment open for Phil Yordan. A
treatment was wanted about the Indonesian volcano, Krakatoa, that
erupted off the coast of Java in 1883, killing thousands. The fee I was
to be paid? $1,000. No other prospects in sight I grabbed it.

One thing more about Lillian. The only one in the studio with
a reputation of being able to handle Cohn, she had a red phone on
her desk, a direct line from his office. While talking to her one day
it went off. She shot two feet into the air.

One of the more fascinating characters of Hollywood lore,
legend followed Phil Yordan wherever he went. Rumored to be
a disbarred lawyer from Chicago, Phil found his way into writing
and producing for Hollywood, was now ensconced at Columbia,
had just written *The Harder They Fall* from a Budd Schulberg novel.
He'd delighted Harry Cohn by trading his salary for points on the
film, which had to be a fool's move, Cohn convinced the film would
not do well. Contrary to Cohn's assessment, it became a major success, Yordan cleaning up far more than his salary would ever have
brought him to Cohn's fury.

Cohn was nothing if not one to get even. As long as Yordan was
through he could leave.

"Fine," Phil replied. "I'll take *Krakatoa* to Fox.

"What's *Krakatoa*?" Cohn wanted to know.

Phil told him.

"Fine," Cohn answered. "You want it? You write it."

Clearly Cohn knew what Phil was up to, that Phil had about as much interest in *Krakatoa* as he did in the lost loves of Mickey Mouse, but Phil needed a treatment, any treatment from anywhere, something to create the illusion he was actually onto something while drawing his salary. Enter me.

The first thing I noticed when I came into Phil's office was the pile of scripts on his desk, and windows! The man had windows! The second was Phil. He had black hair, slicked back, wore rimless glasses, and had a box of expensive Dunhill cigars, none of which he smoked. He chewed them. One end then the other. I liked him, though not everyone did. My old friend Millard Kaufman once told me while working for Phil, he, Millard, became so enraged he literally threw a typewriter at him. I didn't have that experience, but I was warned.

Down the hall from my office was Daniel Fuchs. Danny was a brilliant fiction writer and essayist. We'd become friends during my writing for Schneer. When I told him of my assignment with Yordan, Danny frowned.

"Watch out," he told me, "he'll screw you."

The warning percolated, till one day I confronted Phil with what I'd been told.

Phil stared at me, took off his glasses, laid them on his desk, took the cigar from his mouth.

"Kid," he told me, "I'm gonna screw somebody, it's gonna be a bank."

Most of my story conferences with Phil were listening to him on the phone, purchasing a gas station, selling an apartment building, anything but *Krakatoa*. But he loved to give lessons on screen writing, outrageous as they were.

"Kid," he told me one day, "you got a guy in a snake pit, walls twenty feet high and greased. How do you get him out?"

"How?" I asked.

"Dissolve him out. Audience'll scratch its head and say, well, maybe. Anything else, they'll laugh at you."

Another time, I'd completed the treatment of *Krakatoa*, which Phil read while I sat watching. Finished, he set it down on his desk, a not totally satisfied look on his face.

"You don't like it?" I asked.

"Pretty words, kid."

"But?"

"You ever see Picnic?"

I had. A story about a drifter stopping over in Kansas, stealing the heart of a small town girl. "What'd she see in him, kid?"

I thought about it, pulled out all the psychobabble I could recall from my college drama courses.

"That ain't it, kid," he said.

"Then what?"

"He got a big cock."

As I said, not everybody liked Phil, but he left one mark that writers came to treasure. Serving as a front for friends and other writers blacklisted during the McCarthy era, he moved to Paris, his basement often secretly filled with unemployables working in cubicles. He got the credit, they got the money.

Can't help it. Loved the guy.

A Stone for Benny French

The reception to *Twenty Million Miles To Earth* upon its 1957 release gained for me, for the first time, a toehold on the lower rung of—well, call it tentative credibility. I was not on anyone's "A list", but there were still double bills to fill, and that, for the while, is where I found a tenuous niche.

There was a programmer starring Joel MacCrea and Virginia Mayo. Another for Audie Murphy. B movies at best, for minimum salaries, calling for unrestrained, cliché writing drawn from second rate western novels. At the very least there was food was on the table, house payments were being met, if barely. The diaper service was renewed, and conversation at home was reduced to a manageable volume. Then Vince Fennelly asked to meet.

A former sales manager for Monogram Pictures, Vince had gone into producing. Over lunch he told me what was on his mind. He'd sold a half-hour series to Four Star Television, a Western, *Trackdown*, starring a relatively new actor, Robert Culp, playing a Texas Ranger. Was I interested in coming aboard?

I'd just completed a script for a small movie for Vince, and my continuing prospects in the world of screen writing were shrinking, particularly as the so-called B movie was on its way out. But television? There wasn't a motion picture writer I knew who didn't look down on the medium with contempt. Or fear it. First there was the perceived stigma, especially the shows. Thought to be mostly inconsequential half hours, they had to be written fast, virtually over night, compared to the ten to twenty weeks for a feature.

I ran it past Bette. Having worked in the industry, having seen its insecurities and sometimes cruelties, Bette distrusted it. All and any part of it. If I got an assignment her immediate reaction was, "What about the next one?" It was a question few freelance writers could answer. She came by this fear honestly, having grown up starting out poor with a remarkable father, whom she justifiably worshiped, who'd built himself up from packing lemon crates for Sunkist during the depression to establishing and owning one of the major trucking businesses in Ventura County. Still her fears lingered, not all of which could be blamed on her background. I was not, as I look back on it, reassuring, projecting little confidence.

Nothing else on the horizon, and not having an idea in the world how to do it, I agreed to Vince's offer. What I also didn't know at the time, had no way of knowing, was that Four Star would become my home for the next six years.

The story of Four Star, briefly told, rightly begins and ends with Dick Powell. A respected motion picture actor who longed to direct and produce, Powell saw an opening in the newly born medium of television in 1952. Joining with David Niven and Charles Boyer (there never was a fourth star), Powell, till his death in 1963, built an unrivaled independent television empire. Among the dozen series he would have on the air at one time was a Western anthology, *Zane Grey Theater*, which he hosted. That series gave birth to multiple others, *Trackdown* among them. The writer of his sixty-second weekly introductions? A new discovery Powell brought aboard. Known to Powell as "Skinny", his name was Aaron Spelling.

Working out of my office above Manny Dwork's tailor shop, I reported to Vince as instructed, asked what he had in mind for my first story assignment. Vince had a marvelous way of cocking his head when he heard something idiotic.

"Not quite the way it works," Vince explained. "The *writer* brings in the story."

In all my limited experience writing for the screen I'd worked off someone else's idea, treatment or novel. I'd become, at best, a low level adapter of other people's work, my one sojourn into original material, *Krakatoa*, ending up on the bottom of the pile on Phil Yordan's desk.

Vince liked to solve things over lunch, especially, I'd eventually learn, playing liar's poker to see who'd pay, Vince never losing, due to the fact he had a wallet stacked with bills with unbeatable numbers. Over sandwiches, he got to matters quickly.

"What angers you?" he asked.

"About what?"

"What pisses you off?"

"I don't know."

"Sure you do."

"Cowardice, maybe, I guess."

"Ever gone through it?"

"No," I lied. "No."

Vince's eyebrow was raised as he stared at me. It's what I'd written about in the movie for him.

"Take a shot at it."

"How?"

"You're the writer. That's why you get the big bucks."

$1,500 a script was big bucks? Compared to nothing, yeah, it was. No one had ever asked me to look into myself for a story. In fact, I'd done everything and all to avoid it. *What had my father said? "You haven't got the guts."* I rolled in a sheet of blank paper, spent half a day in thought, headed it with a title, *A Stone for Benny French*.

The story was about Benny French, the lowest member of an outlaw gang left to hold the horses while the rest of the gang raids a bank. Panicking at the first sound of trouble, he drops the reins, scattering the horses, and runs, is tracked down in a sod hut by Culp, the series lead, playing the Texas Ranger, who's pursued him. A desperately poor dirt farmer and his two sons, hearing of the reward on any member of the gang brought in alive, has followed Culp to Benny, the three laying siege, willing to kill Culp to get Benny. What evolves during the night, the two holed up in the hut, is Benny's pathetic history, growing into a relationship with Culp who will not give up Benny even if it means taking on the three armed farmers at dawn. The end has Benny giving up his life to save Culp, thereby becoming the hero he'd always fantasized himself to be.

For the first time in my life I'd put myself on paper. I was Benny French, his history and plight exaggerated, of course, as was his romanticized ending, but I was dealing with feelings of inadequacy, fear and dreams of glory I understood. To my amazement, the character, so intensely drawn, attracted Strother Martin, a remarkable actor to play Benny, Martin, later portraying the warden ("What we have here is a failure to communicate!") in Frank Pierson's *Cool Hand Luke*, starring Paul Newman.

It was more than a beginning. There followed *Fear, Three Legged Fox*, both exploring aspects of myself, and as before attracting the best character actors willing to do television. It got to where Vince barely asked what I was going to do next. When heading off to Hawaii for Christmas, he called me.

"Give me three scripts by the time I get back."

"About what?"

"About thirty pages."

In 1958 Vince ran a spin off on *Trackdown*, *Wanted Dead Or Alive*, about an anti-hero bounty hunter. The lead? Steve McQueen. Writing for the show, I'd never met him, until one day. I was driving over Laurel Canyon on my way to the studio. At the top of the canyon, as I crossed Mulholland, I saw a motorcyclist standing by his bike in some distress. I stopped. It was McQueen. He was out of gas, needed a lift to a station at the bottom of the hill. On the five minute drive down he was silent, till I introduced myself, asked him, "How's the show going?"

"Good."

"Scripts okay?"

"Yep."

"No problems?"

"Nope."

That was Steve, and it showed in his work. Most every other actor I've encountered, once given the script, will underline his or her dialogue, usually in red, some objecting if their dialogue's sparse. Not Steve. He'd give it away. Literally. Not just words, whole speeches. Or lean out those he had to perform. He had a fascination with Gary Cooper's approach to acting. The less he had to say, he believed, the better. His strength? Reacting. That enigmatic smile.

I usually stayed away from the set, but there was something

magnetic about Steve. We all knew it, and sensed we'd better make the best of him as long as we could. He wasn't long for television. I'd just turned up, was standing, watching a take, when Reader, the costume designer, was at my side. He had a stricken look on his face.

"What do you think?" I asked.

"Terrible. Disaster. It's terrible." He was almost crying.

I panicked. "What's wrong?"

"He's wearing the wrong hat!"

Regrettably there's another memory on *Wanted Dead or Alive*, not so pleasant, in fact tragic, that haunts me to this day. I'd been assigned to do a Christmas show for the series entitled *The Eight Cent Reward* about a ten-year-old farm boy who hires McQueen for 8¢, all he has in the world, to find Santa Claus. The idea was simple enough, nothing special, a tear jerker at best. I was working my way through the script one Thursday morning when I received a call from Vince.

"What page you on?"

"Twelve."

Vince never got upset over anything, but he could be firm. He had to have the script by the next morning. It had to be on the stage Monday or he couldn't make the airdate. The director had to have it to prep over the weekend. A half-hour script in those days was thirty-three pages. I was to write twenty-one between then and the next day? How was I to do that?

John Robinson came on the phone. John was Vince's story editor on the show and a good one. Go as far as I could, he told me, then meet him at the studio, he'd work with me through the night.

By the end of day I was on page twenty, exhausted, thirteen pages to go, no energy left, mind mush but I met John as agreed.

"Take one of these," he told me, holding out a pill.

"What is it?"

"Never mind just take it."

A half an hour later I was on fire, flying through dialogue, action, pages. Five in the morning it was finished. I was climbing the walls.

"Take a couple of these," John told me.

"What are they?"

"Just take them."

I did, and came down off the walls with a crash.

The following Monday I went into the office to pick up a copy of my script, and told Verna, Vince's long time secretary, of my night with John.

She stared back at me dolefully. "He does that every day of his life," she told me.

John Robinson, a totally decent, genuinely talented writer, was soon thereafter, I was told, committed to Camarillo State Hospital for the insane.

Jack Lemmon

The studio's prestige show of the late 1950s was the half-hour anthology, *Alcoa-Goodyear*. For reasons unknown to me, the show was finishing up its contractual obligations to Four Star and would be moving over to Screen Gems, a subsidiary of Columbia Studios, the following year. Vince Fennelly was assigned mid-season to take over the remainder of the episodes to be written and filmed. There were several openings left, Jack Lemmon signed for two, having so far turned down what ideas were being offered. Coming off *Mr. Roberts* and *Cowboy*, Jack was a star on the rise. The idea of writing a script for him sent me through the roof.

Every notion I came up with, however, Vince rejected until one day, throwing out a thought as I was leaving his office, Vince yanked me back in. "That's it!"

The story, to be entitled *Loudmouth*, was about just that, a loudmouth, whom we meet at a party, the men loitering before the television to get the latest ball scores. An announcer interrupts to say that there has been a second silk stocking murder in the city, that the police are getting crank calls of false confessions, that anyone caught doing so would be prosecuted. Across the room there's our loudmouth, on the phone, doing just that. The call is traced and he's brought in for questioning, a noose tightening around his neck as the detective builds seemingly circumstantial evidence he can't explain away. That was the original concept.

Then I got a better one. Suppose he'd really done it, really committed those murders. *Was it possible that a killer would actually make such call?*

I met with the Beverly Hills Chief of Police, and to my surprise got his immediate confirmation, that, yes, it was more than possible. "When you commit murder," he told me, "you're God. You've got to tell someone about it, if even in a joke."

I wrote the script in three days and thought it was awful. I didn't even hand it in, I had a messenger deliver it to Vince. The phone rang. It was going to be Vince berating me, asking me what the hell I thought I was doing. It was Jack. He was thrilled, didn't even have to memorize it, he said, it so naturally flowed. The fact that I later received an Emmy nomination was little credit to me. It was Jack, his performance so riveting, he made the words seem more than they were.

Because of *Loudmouth* I was contracted to do three more for *Alcoa-Goodyear*. The second was another for Jack. *Disappearance*. A man and woman, sexually and romantically involved, have plotted to make it appear his very much alive wife has committed suicide, her body apparently lost at sea. When her death is certified, free of suspicion, they then plan to kill her. His wife discovers what they're up to and disappears, deliberately leaving clues that they've murdered her.

There was one deadly scene. When they've set her disappearance in motion, the two have to talk about it to tell the audience what they've done and are intending to do. Talk about a mouthful of exposition. At the cast reading it just lay there like lead. Enter Jack.

"You got a problem with this scene, don't you?" he said over coffee.

"No kidding."

"I'll help you."

Help he did. Playing the dialogue as written, he injected an action not in the script. Just get her into the bedroom, that's all he wants to do as you watch the scene, if he could just get her to shut up, stop talking. The audience heard the words, but Jack brought an element to it that was the focus of attention, giving it humor and suspense. Jack Lemmon. The best, most inventive, contributive actor I ever worked with, and maybe the nicest.

Completing another assignment on *Alcoa-Goodyear* at Four Star, there was still the fourth to write, my contractual agreement inherited by Screen Gems, Bill Sackheim now the executive producer.

Bill was a marvelous talent, a writer-producer with credits that went back to *Playhouse 90*. He also had a clipped, sharp tongue that could lacerate. Try as I did, nothing seemed to please him, nor anything he came up with worked for me, till late one Friday afternoon, growing more and more exasperated, I found a notion that worked for us both. A cop shoots a young gang kid. Did he have to? Or was he just looking for a kill.

"You got it!" Bill pounded his desk. Ten o'clock Monday morning in his office, he told me. "Phones off the hook till we break the story!"

Ten o'clock Monday morning I was there, Bill all but dragging me into his office with great excitement.

"Close the door," he told me!

I closed it.

"Sit down!"

I sat.

"You're not going to believe this!" he said.

I waited to hear how he'd worked out the story. Not quite. On the weekend Bill had played the best game of golf in his life. For the next full hour he took me through every stroke, climbing furniture, make believe whacking the ball out of his closet serving as a sand trap, putting imaginary greens. At eleven o'clock his intercom rang.

"Dailies, Mr Sackheim."

Be back at two o'clock, he told me, which gave me pause. He'd only gone through fourteen holes.

With nothing to do for three hours, I called Nina Laemmle for lunch, met her at DuPars in the Valley. Nina was one of Four Star's two story editors with a special affinity for writers. She was a friend. There was a new production team on the lot, she said over salads. Levy-Gardner-Laven. They had a new series, *Robert Taylor's Detectives*, starring the famed actor. She thought we should meet.

We went to their offices after lunch, mostly just to kill time before reporting back to Sackheim. Nina had done a good selling job. Did I have an idea for their show?

I thought for a moment. "A cop shoots a young gang kid," I told them. "Did he have to? Or was he just looking for a kill."

They bought it on the spot. I never heard from Sackheim, which was a big disappointment. I never found out how he finished his game.

You'll Never Get a Star to Play It

The work at Four Star was constant. Not only *Trackdown*, but soon most of the other shows coming through in the late 1950's. *Zane Grey Theater* was my favorite. For good reason. As an anthology and with Dick Powell's magnetism, stars were drawn to the show most other studios couldn't attract.

I'd written a script for it, *Interrogation*, developed specifically for Powell himself. It was a psychological drama, set in the Mexican-American war, a two-man show, the breaking of a heroic figure without either threat or use of torture. I was on to my favorite theme again, courage vs cowardice. This time in reverse. What could turn a courageous man into a coward with no hint of physical abuse? I was obsessed with the theme, clearly still trying to work out things for myself. Dick refused the part and said we'd never get a star to play it. We got Academy Award nominee Robert Ryan.

"I know what you're asking of me," Ryan told me. "I'll give it to you."

Powell could have buried the show out of pique. He didn't. He took full page ads in the trades recommending it for award consideration. It won the Writers Guild Award that year for Best Written Half Hour Anthology Drama. For writers Four Star was utopia. Writing for the screen as I had, I, as well as most other screen writers I knew, found ourselves cut out of the process the moment our scripts were completed. In television, at least at Four Star, we were part of it all. Budget, location, casting, meeting and working with directors, in on cast readings, the writer and the producer slugging it out together, fighting with advertisers who controlled television in those days, to keep what was written, answerable to no intermediaries, only to the buyer directly. Whoever "they" were who were passing judgment on our material, we met them. You could lose, but it was a head-to-head shootout.

Basically it was because of Dick's chain of command. There was Dick at the top, two story editors under him, one of whom was the beloved Nina Laemmle, whose jobs were mostly to find material and put through contracts. No vice presidents or intermediaries to contend with, no "Head of Development" who would take your idea "upstairs" and translate it wrong. Many writers that came through would become legend. Sterling Silliphant, Robert Towne, Bruce Geller, Gene Roddenberry. And Sam Peckinpah.

Sam had just sold a show, a spin off of *Zane Grey Theater*, entitled *The Westerner*. The pilot, which he wrote and directed, remains to this day the finest half hour of television I've ever seen. It was about a drifter, played by Brian Keith, answering the pleas of the parents of a girl he'd known as a youth. Find her, bring her home. Venturing south to a Texas border town where she'd become a prostitute, in the clutches of an Australian pimp, the Westerner finds the girl desperate, ecstatic to see him. Destroying the pimp in a vicious confrontation, the Westerner sets out to take the girl back to her parents. Except she won't, can't leave, her relationship with the pimp, warped and turgid as it is, being the only security she's known. The Westerner leaves, his mission unfulfilled. When it was over I felt as though I'd been kicked in the stomach.

Sam and I had always hit it off, which was rare for Sam, who could be outrageous and miserable if it pleased him. I never saw it, but the stories about Sam were constant. Years later I was told by producer Kenny Hyman that he, Sam, Jason Robards and John Bryson, the brilliant former cover photographer for *Life* magazine, decided to go duck hunting near Bakersfield. Arriving and taking refuge in duck blinds some fifty yards apart, they encountered a thick Tule fog. With nothing better to do, Sam decided to break the monotony by firing at their voices, buck shot rattling off their blinds to his cackling amusement.

Having seen Sam's pilot at his request, I was asked to work on his show. Meeting in his office we talked, plumbing what might be of mutual interest, discovered we'd both had difficult relationships with our fathers. A story was worked out. The Westerner goes home to see his dying father, the two trying to come to an accommodation before the old man passes away. They can't. It was an idea I anticipated I would likely live out years later at the end of my own father's life. Sam told me to get going on the script. That night my father had a heart attack. That night Sam's father died of a heart attack. The script? It was never written as the network, so unnerved by the public's reaction to Sam's opening show, cancelled it.

It was not the last time Sam Peckinpah and I would cross paths.

This Wasn't Fightin', It Was Fuckin'

It was late 1959 and life was on the march. I had steady employment. My house near the airport purchased in 1954 for $17,400 sold for $19,000, a whopping profit of $1,600. I built a new one in Encino, my three kids, Kevin, Brian and Susan were growing, two already in school—so what was all this talk about a *writers strike*?

Till now I hadn't paid much attention to the Writers Guild. I knew there were two branches, Screen and Television-Radio, each with a separate board and officers, Academy Award-winning screen writer James Webb the overall President. I knew that two separate unions, the old Screen Writers Guild and The Television Writers of America had joined in 1954 to become the Writers Guild of America, much to the distress of many screen writers who, as mentioned before, looked down on television as a second class medium.

I knew, too, that there had been periodic negotiations between the old Screen Writers Guild and Management, minimums established, along with the writers right to determine screen writing credits, as some studios, in the past, had given writing credits to anyone they pleased. But what was all this talk about residuals for reruns on television? A pension plan? A health and welfare plan? Money for screen writers when their movies were sold by studios to the networks for distribution on television?

Management was shocked. *Shocked!* Health plan? Pension plan? What did we think we were, steel workers? An increase in minimums, a few dollars here and there, they might take a look at that. But the rest? No way, not a chance, a total pass!

A full membership meeting was called by the Writers Guild Council, made up of the two separate Boards, the Television Board in particular nervous and fractious. In the audience of about a thousand, our approximate membership at the time, I sat with Bruce Geller, Sam Rolfe and Gene Roddenberry. Soon enough these three would become some of the most prominent, successful writer-producers in television, but not yet, not that day. That day all the leadership could see as they looked down on us were teeth as Nate Monaster, chairmen of the negotiating committee, took us through the Guild's demands and Management's response to them.

What was being called for from the membership was a strike authorization vote, empowering the Council, at its discretion and recommendation of the negotiating committee, to call a strike if Management continued its refusal to bargain in good faith with our union.

Nate held the room, as only he could, as he took us through our proposals, virtually every one of them turned down flat by Management. We listened, but had deep reservations about achieving any success, strike or no strike. I recalled what had happened at Berkeley, how two thousand academics had gone up against *their* management, and had utterly failed over just *one* issue, let alone several.

Questions were fired from the floor.

"What chance of winning do we have?"

"What are the guarantees?"

"If a strike's called, how long will it last?"

"What about those of us on assignments, would we really have to put down our pens as the Guild demands?

"What about those of us with mortgages, kids in private schools, loss of income, those with medical bills or alimony to pay?"

Then a curious thing happened. Jim Webb, Valentine Davies, Charles Brackett and Mel Shavelson rose in support of the authorization request and subsequently doing battle if necessary. Between the four were five Academy Oscars and eleven more nominations. What, someone asked, was in it for them? Why were they supporting this? They were the cream, the most sought after of the industry's writers, could make any deal for themselves they wanted. They didn't need this!

Val Davies, who would later have a Writers Guild award established in his name, answered for them all. "I believe," he said, "it's the responsibility of those of us who find ourselves currently at the top of our profession to lend our support in the fight to achieve gains for you who may not, for the moment, have the power to achieve them for yourselves, as it will be your responsibility in the future to lend your support to those coming along behind you."

A strike authorization was passed almost unanimously. It was a call that quickly morphed into action. Negotiations going nowhere, the Guild called a strike on January 16, 1960, Management regarding the action as bluster, to be short-lived. Finding a bone to be thrown at the writers as a face saving gesture, they let us sweat for a bit, then brought in their best and final offer with slight raises in minimums.

Nate Monaster and his negotiating team rejected the offer hands down. The Council, pushed mainly by the Television Board, ran scared, overruled Nate's committee, approved the contract, took it to the membership for ratification. They didn't bargain on Nate.

I'd never seen him in action before, but I would throughout our relationship, which would prove to be long. Once, several years later, Nate, by then President of the Guild, was in my presence on a telephone call to Bob Lewine of CBS, strongly insisting that a new writer, Bruce Howard, be credited on one of Lewine's shows which was up for Emmy consideration. When Lewine refused, Nate suggested Lewine was opening himself to Guild sanctions.

"Nate," Lewine asked, "are you threatening me?"

"Bob," Nate answered, "of course I'm threatening you."

Responding to the Council's recommendation of the contract offer, Nate addressed the assembled writers.

"I don't dislike this contract," he growled. "I hate it!"

We voted it down. Our own Council had misjudged two things, Nate's leadership, and our resolve, and so had Management which responded with a barrage of contemptuous invective in the press.

There is one thing you never, ever do, and too many in Management have not learned it to this day, I learning it as Management learned it. You do not publicly insult or demean writers, which is what Management did. We are generally an ornery breed. It is a lonely, isolating occupation, and writers don't suffer denigration lightly. Nobody, but nobody in this business starts with what we do. Which is nothing. Or faces what we face. The blank page. Yet few in this business are treated as cavalierly, rewritten, often promiscuously, dismissed, even scorned. One producer told me, "Wait till you have to sit up all night and rewrite these assholes." Ah, that first draft. It's one thing to walk into someone's house and decide to change things around. It's quite another to face a vacant lot.

Why this underlying dismissiveness of writers? Part of the reason is producers and directors, actors too, even some writers who've become producers, are powerless until the script comes in. In that they can't control the writing process, some, not all, but some will try to control the writer. How many directors have to sit and wait in an anteroom, with an appointment, for an hour to see a producer? Walter Newman did. Invited by Paukla-Mulligan, an extremely successful and genuinely honored producing team, to come to their office to discuss a project, Walter, the highly regarded, Academy multi-nominated screen writer, waited forty-five minutes and left. When called, "Where are you, why did you leave?" Walter told them they wouldn't have done that to one of the Three Stooges, and refused to return for a meeting.

The point? Insult, belittle us writers, you do so at your peril. And that's what many in Management did that spring in 1960. We were children, they said, without a clue how the business operated. Some wondered who needed writers anyway? Couldn't the actors just adlib their lines?

Further, it was whispered, there were subversives among us. One Guild writer, sitting in a tight little knot of likeminded, leapt to his feet in a fury during one meeting.

"I know what's going on in this room," he shouted, "and I'm going to the FBI in the morning!"

Rumor had it he did, that our meetings thereafter were infiltrated by Federal agents, never proven, but paranoia was running amuck. The whispering grew louder. We were openly called "pinkos" in the *Hollywood Reporter*, a statement the industry daily was made to retract under threat of suit, all of it only increasing our resolve as Management fired their broadsides.

For me it was Berkeley all over again. Except this time I was in the firefight, not on the sidelines in the cheering section with nothing to lose. Was I frightened, not able to work, no money coming in? To my own amazement, I wasn't. I was energized. For the first time in my life I was a part of something that controlled my destiny, a part of the determining force. It was in my hands, and I liked it.

The strike dragged on. And on. Days into weeks. Weeks into months. Time and time again the Guild Council brought Management's ever-so-slightly improved and final offer to the membership over the negotiating committee's objections. Time and time again we supported Nate and his committee, to such an extent that the membership, all confidence lost in the Television Board, recalled it, literally threw it out of office, sparing no one. On June 10, 1960, six months after going out, Management capitulated. Completely. The result? A double in minimums. A Health and Welfare Plan. A Pension Plan. A royalty plan, which was to be a percentage of producers' revenue, for television reruns, screen writers compensated for the sale of their movies to television.

When the confetti had fallen, and the cheering had grown to a manageable din, Charles Brackett rose to bestow his immortal benediction. "This wasn't fightin'" he grinned. "It was fuckin'."

Lover, I Need a Bottle Show

With the impeachment of the entire Television Board, a new one had to be formed. Guild President Jim Webb asked me to run.

I'd only met Jim once before, but I'd apparently made an impression with an absolutely chance piece of luck. I'd been assigned to a Guild credit arbitration panel before the strike which Jim was chairing, my first involvement ever with the Guild. Two writers were both claiming original authorship of a screenplay. One was lying, one was telling the truth. How to figure it out? We wracked our brains, coming up with nothing, until I had a thought. We called the two writers in separately. There was a number on the lead character's apartment door in the script. How had each come up with it? Writer A said he'd made it up, a random choice. Writer B said it was his own apartment number, showed us his driver's license to prove it. Writer B got the credit. Writer A got a severe reprimand. Jim was impressed, and so the invitation to run. I did, and won a seat on the Television Board.

Nevertheless work was of primary concern. The strike had drained our savings. Along with the vast majority of Guild members I was broke. I needed $2,000 till I could get back to writing, and the only one I knew whom I could go to for it was my Father.

I'd never asked for nor borrowed money from him, nor received any, not since leaving for Berkeley twelve years before and I didn't want to have to start now. While I was struggling in the early 1950s, our relationship had begun to grow less confrontational as a sort of resignation set in toward my mediocrity. As I began to achieve a modicum of success it all changed. The old tensions returned. The more success I achieved the more judgmental he became.

"It seems to me," he would criticize, "your friends aren't going anywhere."

Or, "I don't mind you not calling me, but for you not to call your Mother!"

He and Mother had moved from Santa Monica to a lesser but still luxurious house off Sunset Boulevard in the Palisades. Having phoned that I was coming, I arrived to find them packing, the house up for sale. My father's twenty year tenure at Metro had ended, the studio downsizing, no longer in the business of hiring contract producers. The new house they'd be going to, I reasoned, would be smaller, less a financial drain considering their new circumstances. Mother, I knew, could adjust, but Dad?

"So where you moving to?" I asked him, guessing Westwood.

"Burgenstock."

"Where?"

"Switzerland."

"What's there?"

"Audrey and Mel."

Audrey Hepburn and Mel Ferrer. Dad had a way of running to celebrities whenever his world imploded.

"For how long?"

"Six months. We've taken a villa."

A villa? In Burgenstock? A village located in the hills above Lake Lucerne, with five star hotels and restaurants? Six months? He'd just lost his job at Metro. How were they going to pay for it?

I soon learned how. Instead of taking his sizeable pension, paid out monthly for the rest of his life, Dad had taken it all in one lump sum.

This kind of extravagance was nothing new. Every year a new car. A closet filled with twenty suits, two dozen coats and trousers, all made from imported English and Italian fabrics by a personal tailor who turned up at the house at least once a month. Shoes from McAfee of London, all shaped and formed from personal lasts on file with the company. A wine cellar rivaling most restaurants. A live-in maid. A nurse for the children when we were little. Once a chauffeur. There had even been a time when Mother took her treasured sterling silverware, inherited from her mother, to Jerome Kern's house, hiding it from Dad, to keep him from selling it on a whim so they could take a trip to Paris. Highly salaried at Metro he lived check to check, his business manager too often calling with, "Need money!" It was as though profligate spending, and his ability to do so, was a measure of his self-worth.

I tried to reason with him, suggesting Burgenstock might not be the wisest choice for the moment, especially for Mother who was not all that great in altitude, trying to mask my worry with humor, which he saw through, flashing anger.

"Your mother and I have an understanding!" he said sharply.

You didn't tell Dad how to run his life. Nobody did, whatever the cost to anyone else. So off to Burgenstock they went, Mother unwilling or unable to deny him. In six months his pension was gone. Every last cent of it.

The $2,000 borrowed from him was paid back quickly when, following the strike, Dick Powell invited me to go under contract, a two-year guaranteed deal worth more than I'd ever made or could make freelancing.

Relinquishing my room above Manny Dwork's tailor shop, I moved onto the Four Star lot, was given an office and a secretary, a marvelous, newly married young Canadian, Diane Kelleher, who would, down the line, rescue me from a disaster. The ink wasn't dry on my name plate before Aaron Spelling, who'd taken over as producer of *Zane Grey Theater*, called me to his office.

"Lover," he addressed me in a greeting he used for all, "I need a bottle show, two people in one room, if you could come up with such a thing, a budget saver."

I had an idea, loosely inspired by that fishing trip I'd taken with my Egyptian friend while at Berkeley in 1950, the two of us so quickly solving the break out of the Egyptian-Israeli war.

The American Civil War, I told Aaron. Two patrols, one North, one South, find themselves stranded, lost and starving, each separately sending out a marksman, both little more than boys, to find food. Snow begins to fall, the first of the season, when each comes upon a cow near an old abandoned sod hut. Simultaneously shooting the cow, each claims it as his. Wary of each other, ready to kill each other, the two take refuge in the hut as the snow builds. There a Bible is found. In it is written a warning. If caught here when the first snows fall, say your prayers, there's no way out till spring. Faced with certain starvation and death, the two work out the entire North-South problem during the night, find, in the morning, the sun out, the snow stopped. Old hatreds return, and with it their ownership of the dead cow. They fight over it, kill each other.

Aaron was enthusiastic, said he'd run it past Dick Powell, knew Powell would approve it, would notify the story department and have a contract put through. We settled on a title, *Silent Sentry*. A pretty straightforward assignment. Stay tuned.

Aaron taking over the show wasn't the only change at the studio. No longer was it to be just Dick Powell, his two story editors, his producers and writers. Tom McDermott, head of broadcast programming at the Madison Avenue advertising agency, Benton and Bowles, who had successfully done business with Four Star, made a suggestion to Powell. Powell's first love was making movies? Go make them. He, McDermott, would come west, run Four Star for him. Powell bought it, brought McDermott to Four Star and gave him the reins.

Tom McDermott was not a dilettante. He had a legitimate record selling successful shows. Other than that, he was everything Powell was not. The first thing he did was bring in a platoon of executives whose functions were hard to define. This was nothing new. I'd seen it happen before and would again, executives bringing in a raft of VP's, most unnecessary, to enhance the appearance of their authority and power. In Tom's case, one was worth his salt, very much so, Dominick Dunne, who would one day make his mark as one of America's leading investigative journalists. He was approachable, collaborative and knowledgeable about storytelling and writing.

McDermott was not. Selling a show and making it were two separate functions. I found him aloof and competitive, and I wasn't alone. Tell him an idea you had for a new series, he'd more often than not answer with, "Yeah, I had that idea myself last week." But he had the job and in the beginning delivered, selling a collection of new series, most of which were short-lived.

Never personally comfortable around McDermott, perhaps out of resentment of his authority replacing Powell's, I settled on working directly with the producers, giving McDermott a wide berth, leaving studio politics to others. Work there was. The strike over, there was pressure to get scripts written and quickly, among them a pilot for Aaron, a half-hour anthology starring Lloyd Bridges playing a reporter insinuating himself weekly into the role of the character he was investigating.

We needed a sponsor, and didn't have one, till one day Aaron and I were summoned to McDermott's office. Seated there was a man in his late seventies, rumpled black suit, tie askew. It was Henry Kaiser, billionaire American industrialist who'd become known as the father of modern American ship building. He owned a half-hour on air and the studio wanted it.

Aaron and I began to sell the Bridges show, pitching our hearts out, McDermott pumping encouragement behind Kaiser, the old man glancing at his watch, looking on dolefully like he'd rather be any place else, when Dick Powell entered the room. He'd come on the lot to do a cameo on one of his shows. There was tissue under his collar, full make up on his habitually tanned, handsome face. He came in with that characteristic smile and jaunty walk, asking how things were going, just wanting to say hello. Then his arms were around Aaron's and my shoulders. We were his boys, and anything we said we could do we could do, he told Kaiser, and then an anecdote full of famous names and Kaiser wasn't looking at his watch anymore. Ten minutes later when Powell returned to the set, Kaiser and Four Star were partners, the show on the air. But not before a bizarre moment with Bridges.

Assembling three days before the start of production, we gathered about the table ready for a cast reading. All of us, that is, except Lloyd. As he opened his script, we stared in disbelief. The entire teleplay had been rewritten on the blank, left side of each page. Not just Lloyd's dialogue, but everyone else's as well, no warning, no call from Lloyd that he had problems with the material. Aaron and I, the director and supporting cast were stunned. The script had been approved by the network, Lloyd had approved it.

Challenging him about the changes, Lloyd seemed to have a difficult time explaining why they'd been made, but defended them as though defending his wife, which he was. The rewrite had been done by her. Later I would learn from Ellis Marcus, story editor on a series at MGM, he'd run into the same thing with Lloyd, had handled the problem the same way we did that day. Maybe, it was suggested, Lloyd would be happier not doing the show, which was a pretty chancy threat. The series was entitled *The Lloyd Bridges Show*. Fortunately however that ended it, no further talk of rewrites mentioned. Lloyd Bridges. One of the most decent people I ever worked with. And one of the most difficult.

When the series made it to the network's fall schedule, which should have been the happy conclusion, McDermott called Aaron and me into his office.

"Boys," he said, "got this little problem. I've given away 115 percent of the show." You could cut the gloom with a knife as we heard, "We going to get reasonable, or do I pull it?" The "we" of course was Aaron and I. Exit our profit positions, at least mine.

But there was still *Silent Sentry* to write for Aaron, and it began to occur to me weeks had gone by and I'd yet to see a contract. Maybe Powell hadn't approved it after all. I called Nina Laemmle in the story department, asked why a contract hadn't gone through.

Nina seemed surprised. *Silent Sentry?* A contract *had* gone through. To Aaron. It was his. He said so. He was writing it.

I called Aaron's office. He didn't take the call. Called again. Same thing. I called him at home, got him on the phone as he answered it. What the hell was going on? I asked. It was *my* story, *I* brought it to him, and *he* was writing it?

Aaron exploded. Typical goddamn writer, he ranted. Tell him an idea you've got for a story and the next thing he's trying to steal it! He thought I was different from the rest, I wasn't! Thought I could be trusted, I couldn't! Shows you never, ever tell an idea to another writer till it's on paper, happens every damn time!

For three days I went over and over it in my mind.

Was he right? Aaron's conviction, his outrage had been so dominant. Was it really his idea all along? Had I fantasized that it was based on that college experience I'd had with my Egyptian friend? Once hearing it, liking it, did I really think it was mine? Sometimes when hired to do a rewrite, writers, retyping someone else's original, will convince themselves they invented the whole thing themselves. Was that, in its way, what happened?

My doubt grew. I decided to let it go. Or try to. It was spring, 1961, and fortuitously a diversion arrived. A huge one. *The Dick Powell Show*, sold to NBC. It was to be an hour-length anthology, with a high cast budget and Powell's agreement to appear in at least one out of every four.

Throughout Powell's career he'd had unparalleled success. He was television's top male star, president of its leading, most productive independent production company, and a millionaire several times over. What he felt he had never had, what he wanted desperately, more than even producing or directing movies, was personal critical acclaim, not for the work of others, but for himself. This show could, and would, get it for him. Returning full time to the lot, he moved virtually all else aside to see that it did so. The show, in effect, became his show. He was its executive producer, its soul, and nothing happened on it he didn't know about.

"If my aunt in Little Rock doesn't understand it, it doesn't go on my show," he'd say.

Except he couldn't make it stick, and that is what made the two years on *The Dick Powell Show* among the most rewarding I experienced.

When you had a story, you went in with a producer, or you went in alone, but the story was always cleared with Powell directly. He would sit behind his desk, phones turned off, and listen intently as long as you wanted to talk, mentally recording what you had to say with absolute concentration. He could, and did, when you were done, tell back to you what you had told him so you knew you'd been heard, and accurately. If he liked the idea, that was it. You went away and you wrote. If he didn't like it, or didn't understand it, ("If my aunt in Little Rock . . . .") that's where the fun could start.

Basically Powell was a simple man, politically conservative, steeped in traditional values. And there he sat, facing impassioned, young, mostly Jewish writers, wanting to deal with confounding themes that made up the world we saw and not from behind a millionaire's desk.

I only got mad at him once.

"Dammit," he said, after reading a script I'd written, "I can picture Khrushchev reading this and just loving it."

He only got mad at me once.

"Dammit," I said, after he wanted his character changed in another script I'd written, "the story's the star of this script, Dick, not you."

I've heard that Powell never met a man he couldn't forgive. It took all he had to keep his record clean on that one.

But the point of it is, as much as he wanted to honor his aunt in Little Rock, he honored us more. If you fought for your story, if you really believed in it, showed by your presentation and conviction that you believed in it, and he believed in you, he'd let you do it. Often not understanding it, not confident of it, he'd let you do it.

The show had its traditionals, its slick melodramas and mysteries, but also ran off with the Writers Guild top television anthology awards both years it was on the air, as well as other nominations and a trunk full of critical acclaim.

We did shows that took place in Italy, on island prisons, in Spain and Malaysia, and we did them on the lot, supported by a superb production team Powell had built that told you how you *could* do it, not how you could *not*.

One such show was *Death in a Village* which I wrote for Aaron, our past conflict over *Silent Sentry* put to rest. Taking place in Spain, it was the story of a former bullfighter, played by Gilbert Roland, who'd showed cowardice in the ring. Running from his past, he'd become a priest, finds himself assigned to a small, dirt poor village in the Spanish mountains. The town, he soon discovers, has been paying tribute to a murderous gang of mountain raiders, giving up its young men to replenish the gang in favor of occasional food and supplies. In short order the priest finds himself in the ring again to face his fears or run again.

Cowardice, courage. Again that theme. You'd think it would get old. It hadn't. It was as though I was still searching, still trying to find some truth in myself I hadn't resolved. There was a poem I'd read in college by Kipling. *Tomlinson*. Dying, Tomlinson presents himself to both afterlife courts of judgment, relates, when queried, all he has heard, read, thought, observed. But what has he *been*, what acts of nobility or chance has he *taken*? Left with nothing on which to judge him, he's denied both heaven and hell, returned to earth, there to roam as a nonentity, a nonperson, a cipher. *Was that the course I was on? Or through the lead character in Death in a Village was I delving into myself?*

When the script was turned in, Aaron did two things. He signed on one of the best television directors in the business, Don Medford, and sent the script to Cecil Smith, television critic of the *Los Angeles Times*, who wrote a glowing piece about it.

Then everything fell apart. Don called me into his office. He was withdrawing from the project as director. He loved the script, but he was withdrawing. His reason? It was four days to go before production, a complicated piece to do, and he couldn't get Aaron to address budget, sets, costumes, casting, nothing. In fact he couldn't even get him on the phone or find him, till rumored he was off somewhere in Los Angeles Harbor on a photo op with his then wife, actress Carolyn Jones. Don simply wasn't going to get blamed for ruining what he considered a fine piece of work.

Don's withdrawal sickened me. Not Aaron. He simply found another director willing to go through the motions. Which is what he did, no attention to detail, theme or nuance. The result was terrible. Stagnant, plodding, nothing realized. Cecil Smith wrote another column in the *Times* saying so after the show was broadcast, wondering what could have gone so wrong.

In all honesty, having worked with Aaron over the years, despite his incredible successes, detail, theme and nuance were never his strong suits. I'll amend that. They were never his suits at all. What were, were simple uncomplicated concepts. *Love Boat. Fantasy Island. Beverly Hills 90210.* Mind candy, he called them. He was also a genius at casting. Others, myself included, would pass on an actress or actor, thinking their skills might not be good enough for what was called for. Aaron would not only sign them, but would cast them in leading roles where they became television stars, instinctively knowing their personalities and appeal were what the public would respond to. No one, but no one was as good at that as he was. How to put together a show like *Death in a Village* however? Not a thought. Though later it would win a Writers Guild nomination for Best Written Anthology, judged solely on the merits of the writing.

Meanwhile, I was preparing another for the Powell Show, Aaron again to produce, a much simpler story, a mystery, when I got a call from the William Morris Agency. On the phone was an agent I knew and respected. Was *Silent Sentry* my story, he asked. For a moment I couldn't input what he was talking about. He explained. He had a client who'd pitched a concept to Aaron for *Zane Grey Theater*. It wasn't the same as *Silent Sentry*, but there were similarities in that it dealt with two patrols, one Southern, one Northern, during the Civil War, both taking refuge in a cave one night. Did Aaron rip him off, the writer wanted to know. Calling Aaron about it, the agent was told, "No, no, lover, that was Chris Knopf's story. He and I had an understanding. I'd write that one, because I gave him an idea for a pilot which he would write."

Understanding? What understanding? It was utter bull. Every word of it!

I called for a meeting with Powell, and learned what happened.

Aaron had gone to the set where Dick was working to clear the project, told the idea to Powell who liked it, a lot, asked Aaron where he'd gotten it. Aaron couldn't resist. "It's mine," Aaron told him.

I was furious, told Powell I wasn't writing for Aaron again.

"Okay. Why not?"

"Because he's a lying, cheating, thieving . . . ."

Powell nodded. "You're right."

I couldn't believe what I'd just heard. "Then why the hell have you got him around here?" I asked.

"I'll tell you why," he answered. "While the rest of you guys are trying to win awards, he's keeping me on the air."

It was true. Bruce Geller, Dick Simmons and I, all working on *The Dick Powell Show*, were trying to do just that, and admittedly having success at it. Aaron was pouring out episodes. One after another. Feeding those hungry, relentless hours on television. It became Aaron's signature. Taking the long view of his industry accomplishments, no one, but no one achieved the massive amount of output as Aaron. If at times he was sacrificing quality with his so-called mind candy fantasies, I truly don't think it was a cynical choice. Raised on Browder Street, in Dallas, Texas, a slight, frail kid, he told me more than once his day was made if he could get to school and back without being beaten up. Maybe he was running from Browder Street with those shows. Maybe they were him.

With that background I would have thought he would be super-sensitive to others. If he was, it didn't always come out that way. I'd arrived in his office at Four Star one day when he put down a script he'd been reading, shook his head.

"Boy, what a piece of shit," he said. He must have seen my shiver. "What's wrong?"

"Do you know what a writer hears when you say that?"

"What?"

"That *he's* a piece of shit."

"No, no, lover," he objected, "I was talking about the script, not him."

"What do you think a script is?" I asked. "Good or bad, it's a writer's thoughts, his feelings. It's him."

With it all, he was extremely protective of himself, with an instinct for self preservation. I was in his office once again, going over a script I'd written, when his secretary told him Hubbell Robinson was there to see him. Aaron blanched. Robinson was west coast head of CBS at the time, a very major player.

"What's he want?" Aaron asked me.

I shrugged. What did I know?

Aaron told his secretary to send Robinson in, at the same time reached into his desk for a pair of dark glasses, put them on. When Robinson entered and it was determined that his visit was purely social, Aaron removed the glasses, instinctively knowing he could hide any apprehension with his infectious smile, but not his eyes. I put that moment in the script I was writing for him. He never noticed.

Another time years later, I was in his sumptuous office on Wilshire Blvd where he was holding court with several of us (yes, I was working with him again), and he brought up *Silent Sentry*. It was his favorite story, maybe his best, he told the room, as I watched him with bemused amazement. Having said it so many times over the years he'd come to believe it. He once told me, with a sort of vulnerable grin, "I've lied so many times in my life, I can't remember *what* the truth is anymore."

Just Like Oswald, Not Even A Trial

True to my word, I sought out and found another producer on the lot who proved, not only to be extraordinary, but became a life long friend.

The Dick Powell Show was into its second year, and working on it now with Stan Kallis reenergized me. The show got ratings and envy. And then we got wind of something that made none of it worthwhile. We heard Dick was sick. There were a lot of rumors as to what it was, but the one word, cancer, kept coming up.

If Powell was sick, you couldn't prove it by him. He'd reunited with his estranged wife, June Allyson, had sailed off with her on his yacht during the summer, and now was returned. He looked great, and acted it, and fought you tooth and nail in those meetings, testing your will, yielding to it as usual if he felt your own sincere devotion to your project.

He was dying. He knew it and we didn't and he never told us nor gave us the slightest indication of it, nor a single moment's sense that he was hiding that hideous truth, that within several months he'd be gone. And then he was. January 2, 1963. Singer, actor, producer, director, sailor, pilot, born in Mountain View, Arkansas, he was fifty-eight years old.

The pall that set over Four Star was palpable. And over me

a near disaster. Arriving home one night I found a letter from George Elber, Four Star's resident counsel who'd been brought in by McDermott. Having co-authored the pilot of a now on-air series entitled *Target The Corrupters* about an investigative reporter, I'd written an episode dealing with the plight of migratory workers. The letter from Elber stated a newspaper journalist from The Long Island Bee was initiating a plagiarism suit against Four Star for having ripped off his article as the basis of my script. As I was the author, Elber pronounced, the suit was being passed on to me. I, in effect, was the one who was liable.

In fact, I *had* used the article in my research, employing certain facts and elements from it cataloging specific abuses to migratory workers along the eastern seaboard. If what Elber was saying in that letter was true, I was in terrible trouble, Elber making clear the studio had no intention whatsoever of hiring or paying attorneys to fight the suit on my behalf.

Ah, but Diane Kelleher, my young Canadian secretary. Diane never threw anything away. Not even notes I'd written on paper napkins. Digging through her files she found it. An inter office communiqué from Four Star studio executive, Dominick Dunne, bringing the newspaper article to my attention, telling me I was free to use any part of it if of use. So the suit was thrown right back in the studio's lap. It went bananas.

I was called to McDermott's office, found him there with Elber. If there was anyone I was less enamored with than McDermott it was George Elber. It had gotten back to me he had said I was a deadbeat, coming, I suspected, from McDermott. This after writing or rewriting for the company four pilots to date that had made it to network series, a couple of dozen scripts for various shows, an Emmy nomination and three Writers Guild nominations, one winning. Nor was I the only one being so disparaged. Nearly every one brought in by Powell before McDermott's arrival was the butt of his scorn.

But this time there was nothing like that. Given coffee and Danish, I faced smiles all around. Elber took charge.

"You have Nick's note?"

"I do."

"May I see it?"

I handed it over. It was written in long hand, signed by Dominick on his personalized inter office note paper.

"This is a copy, a Xerox," Elber told me.

"It is."

"May I see the original?"

"It's at my lawyer's." I didn't have a lawyer, but Elber's "Ah ha!" confirmed he didn't know that.

I would, of course, testify on the studio's behalf, Elber purred, acknowledging that writers always, as a matter of course, felt free to use factual articles from magazines and newspapers as legitimate source material, right?

No, I told Elber, *not* right. Writers would only do so if the studio's legal department cleared such material first or initiated it, which in this case it had done. The smile froze on Elber's face. He looked to McDermott who was looking at me. Tom thanked me, a clear invitation to leave, but the look on his face said there'll be another day.

The suit was dismissed out of hand before it ever got to court, but otherwise things were growing sticky at Four Star. With no Dick Powell to run interference, shows began to wane and crumble, McDermott having sold, but not having sold wisely. There was a pilot with ABC starring Joan Crawford, which was proving a cost overrun nightmare, the show never making it to the network schedule. Bruce Geller and Bernie Kowalski sold one, for which I wrote a script, about the government's Health and Welfare Department, staring Robert Taylor, that was scheduled, then cancelled before it went on air due to content considered too politically liberal for the network to live with.

Then something that paled everything else. November 22, 1963. Bruce Geller, Dick Simons and I were walking back from the studio cafeteria when someone told us, running by, President Kennedy had been shot. The only television set on the lot we knew of was in Jackie Cooper's office. Twenty of us crowded in, all convinced that that was the end of Goldwater who'd announced he was running for the presidency against Kennedy, that clearly some right wing nut case had to have done this –– when we heard it. Kennedy was dead. The world stopped.

For four days, through the tragic sight of Jackie Kennedy, Johnson's oath of office, the capture of Oswald, Jack Ruby shooting him in public view, Kennedy's coffin transported down Constitution Avenue to the Capitol Rotunda, I never left my television. Until there was a clang and a clatter in the cul de sac outside my house. Running to the front door, I looked out at my eleven year old son, Kevin. Tossing a football around with a friend, he'd knocked over our mail box. Pent up with emotion, I took it out on him. What the hell did he think he was doing? Didn't he know what those things cost?

"Can I explain?" he asked.

"No!"

"Just like Oswald," he answered. "Not even a trial!"

Time began to heal, as it does, and work filled the void. But Kennedy remained on my mind. I developed a series concept which, when completed, I took to McDermott for presentation to a network. Called *The Cannons Of San Francisco*, it dealt with a family, not unlike the Kennedys, involved in industry and banking in the 1850s, one of the most colorful periods in California history, given the gold rush, the establishment of Pacific shipping, the arrival of gangs, the Sidney Ducks, expelled from Australia, the influx of Chinese Coolie labor brought in to build railroads, as well as the establishment of Chinatown.

McDermott turned it down. I wasn't asking him to approve it, I told him, I was asking him to take it to the networks. Let *them* turn it down if it wasn't something they wanted. McDermott held firm, and I soon discovered why.

A concept had been brought into the studio which was being set up at CBS, entitled *The Big Valley*. Though taking place about the same time in the San Joaquin Valley, the concept was close enough to mine that McDermott was going with a bird in the hand, did not want my project muddying the waters. Furthermore, he wanted me to write the *The Big Valley* pilot.

I was livid. Especially, once reading the presentation, which is all that existed. I felt it had no "legs" as they say, and told McDermott so, and turned it down, McDermott telling me as I left his office, "You're going to write it!" Where this was going I had no idea. But not one I was likely to win.

Morale on the lot was sinking, and not just mine. Dick Simmons, who, among us all, seemingly had the best relationship with McDermott, would one day soon be forcibly ejected from the studio for turning down a pilot McDermott wanted *him* to write. Bruce Geller and Bernie Kowalski, also under contract, wanting out but unable to get their release, rejected anything McDermott told them to do, as he rejected whatever they brought to him.

It was a standoff, but not a total waste of time. In Bruce and Bernie's office was a continual game, often played for money, throwing metal push pins, like mini-darts, at a cork board. The trick was to get them to stick. We got pretty good at it, Bernie, the gambler in the crowd, giving me five to one odds I couldn't throw and stick five push pins all at once with one throw. I won.

Finally McDermott had had all he could take, summoned Kowalski and Geller to his office.

"Bruce, you two," McDermott unloaded, pointing a finger, "sit around doing nothing, playing darts all day, Bruce, just stealing my money..."

To which Bernie interrupted. "Tom. I'm Bernie. *He's* Bruce."

It was my turn now, and McDermott was not about to suffer any more fools. I was to write the script of The Big Valley, he told me, starting now.

"Bars off the shoulders?" I asked him.

"Go ahead."

For the next fifteen minutes I unloaded. He hadn't the vaguest notion how to work with talent, I told him. He didn't know story, how to communicate with his people, took credit for anything that worked, never blame for what didn't. He was head of the greatest independent studio so far devised, made up of some extremely talented people, and all anyone wanted was to get the hell out.

He listened with utter lack of emotion till I was through.

"You finished?"

"Yeah."

"How long will it take you to write Big Valley?"

"I'm not going to do it."

"Then you're on suspension."

Levy-Gardner-Laven, producers of the project, called me to their offices. Jules, Arthur and Arnold. Three of the nicest, most sympathetic, decent producers I ever worked for, having written for them before, *The Rifleman*, and *Robert Taylor's Detectives*. They calmed me down and asked what it would take to get me to write the pilot. I was ready for the question and answered. Get me out of my contract with Four Star, pay me $10,000 and I'll do it, with one proviso. That I get to bring my characters from my project into the script. They went to McDermott with my proposals which were granted. I wrote the pilot, agreeing to write the second show as well if it sold so that the two could be linked together for an overseas motion picture sale.

The script was turned down by CBS for whom it was developed, but picked up by ABC, Barbara Stanwyck signed to play the head of a major ranching family in the Valley, one son a lawyer, another a rancher running the immense spread, a third entering the picture during the pilot as the bastard son of their now dead father, and a free spirited daughter.

Inevitably when young actors arrived at a studio, especially those with their first series assignment, the first thing they'd do is scope the landscape, see which actors on other shows had their own trailer, with a refrigerator, maybe a television set. Stanwyck would have none of it. She was the first on the set every morning, knew her lines, never complained, set such a high standard of behavior the rest fell quickly in line.

Having been a major movie star, Stanwyck had worked on some of the best material by some of the industry's finest writers. So writing for her was daunting, but she knew how to get the best, certainly out of me.

At the end of each show, in the beginning at least, Stanwyck assembled her series family and offered a homily summing up what they'd all gone through. I'd completed the second episode when she summoned me to the set. She was dressed in her blue pinafore, looking lovely and trim. She took me aside. She had the second script, opened to the last page. Barbara was a stomach poker when she talked, so you always had to brace around her so she wouldn't hit flab.

"Christopher," she said, poking my braced stomach, "I've just read this closing speech you've written for me. It's so beautiful I want to be certain I get it right. Would you take me through it?"

I started to do so, realizing as I did, I didn't have a clue what it was about. I'd written it late at night to get the script in. I began to ad lib my way into another approach.

"I wonder," she said, poking again before I could brace, "if you'd put it in just those words for me."

What she'd done, rather than challenging the speech as the bunch of nonsense it was, which she certainly could have done, was to get me to rethink it, and saved my ego. A totally gracious lady, and a forever memory, but she could be bawdy.

I was in Arthur Gardner's office one day when Barbara walked in from the set, flopped down on the couch, dropped her feet on the coffee table, propped the newly delivered script on her lap.

"Arthur," she said as we waited to see what was coming, "I'm sick and tired of these fucking homilies." Never another one written.

It was the end of my employment at Four Star. Six years. As for Four Star, at the time of Dick Powell's death it had a dozen shows on the air, give or take one. Two years later it had two. A year after that just one, *The Big Valley*, which played on ABC for four seasons.

The 800-Pound Gorilla

He was slight, trim suited, seemingly inoffensive, in his thirties, innocuous, soft spoken. The sort who might pass by unnoticed, pencil in hand, hurrying from one hurry to another. In fact, he was an eight hundred pound gorilla, and he carried a very big club.

His name was Carl Perian, staff director, Subcommittee to Investigate Juvenile Delinquency, United States Senate. Hearings were currently being held in Washington D.C., under the chairmanship of Senator Thomas Dodd of Connecticut, looking into the "Effects on Young People of Violence and Crime Portrayed on Television." Nate Monaster and I were now President and Vice-President of the Television Branch of the Writers Guild. What was wanted from Nate and me was for the two of us to fly to Washington and testify before the Committee.

Lions of the Senate, waking up to the public's interest, scrambled for seats on the Committee like a game of musical chairs. Network presidents were summoned to testify under oath, subpoenaed if they refused. Studio heads, among them Tom McDermott of Four Star, were called. Violence on television was desensitizing and destroying our children, and Washington wanted an accounting of who was responsible for it.

The root cause everyone knew was ratings. Sex and violence

got them. Still, as witnesses paraded before the Committee, no one took responsibility. Networks blamed advertisers, advertisers blamed sponsors, sponsors blamed studios, studios blamed their producers who blamed the networks. Ivan Tors, producer of *Sea Hunt*, under questioning by Perian, (Congressional Record S. Res. 48, Part 10) passed the blame on to writers:

MR. PERIAN: Do you feel it is possible...with the situation which exists...to have a constructive show...during the so-called prime time hours?

MR. TORS: Yes, but...the easiest way to get an audience is with violence because it doesn't take much thinking. I would say with brutality and violence...the writers have no other ideas.

Walter Scott, Executive Vice-President of NBC got in his licks.

MR. SCOTT: It was our experience that most of the excesses stemmed either from opportunistic sensationalism or a poverty of invention. By that I mean that some writers use violence as padding or a crutch in place of story telling resourcefulness.

Going to Washington to testify was not an eager prospect. First, and foremost, we were being asked to point fingers at our own employers, present, past and future, and to do so publicly. Second, and this applied to me solely, two shows were being featured as examples of excessive violence. One was the pilot episode of *Target*,

The Corrupters, of which I, being the last of three writers, shared credit. The principal offense in the show, entitled *Million Dollar Dump*, dealing with mob control and corruption in big city garbage collection, was an ugly scene in which a body is thrown into and crushed in a dumpster.

I had inherited that scene, as well as others, when assigned as the final writer to bring the show's characters and dialogue to life. In a meeting with Ackerman and Burrows, the producers, I expressed my dismay, asked that the scene be deleted. To which Burrows replied, "Ooo guy no, that's neat!" Under interrogation by Dodd's special counsel, Paul Laskin, McDermott corroborated my concern.

MR. LASKIN:	Were you aware of the scene from other members of Four Star, or from Burrows and Ackerman?
MR. MCDERMOTT:	We had several discussions of this when we were shooting. Our writer raised the issue with Burrows and Ackerman.
MR. LASKIN:	What was the point made by the writer?
MR. MCDERMOTT:	He questioned it.
MR. LASKIN:	What was the reaction of either Mr. Burrows or Mr. Ackerman?
MR. MCDERMOTT:	They thought it should be shot and it was shot.

Nate and I consulted and met with Perian. We agreed to testify, with two provisos. We were not volunteering to go, but would be subpoenaed. Second, I would not be interrogated about my participation in *Target The Corrupters*, as that would involve citing people I was working with and for. Perian agreed to both without objection.

Dodd's hearings were being held in the Old Senate Office Building, made famous by Joseph Welch and Joe McCarthy. Entering, I saw the room was packed with industry elite, but mostly reporters suffering day after day of "non mea culpa" testimony, and there we sat at the witness table, Nate and I, facing dour, scornful senators. Tom McDermott, preceding us, true to his nature had turned Dodd testy. Eugene Gleason, investigator, had interrogated.

MR. GLEASON:	You mean these (scripts for "Target, The Corrupters") are based on fact?
MR. MCDERMOTT:	Well, the background is fact.
MR. GLEASON:	It was not a fact that a man was in real life shot by two guns with silencers on, and dumped over a hill and burned.
MR. MCDERMOTT:	No. The basic material...
MR. GLEASON:	Isn't it enough that he was dead? Did he have to be burned, too?
MR. MCDERMOTT:	I guess for him it was enough that he was dead.
CHAIRMAN DODD:	What are you trying to do? Do you think that it is important that you show this kind of violence in order to convince people that there has been corruption?

And the Chairman wasn't through. Quoting from a McDermott interview with the *Fresno Bee*:

CHAIRMAN DODD: "Pulling no punches, McDermott refers to some hearings and statements of politicians as nonsense and headline hunting." Do you really believe this is just a headline hunting procedure here?

Of course it was, and everyone knew it, but no one, not even McDermott, dared say so. Concluding his testimony, McDermott was smoldering as he withdrew and Dodd moved on to us. Sworn in, we were turned over to Carl Perian. Immediately Perian repeated NBC Executive VP Walter Scott's testimony condemning writers' use of violence as a crutch, asking Nate to comment. I had the sudden feeling we were there to be star witnesses.

MR. MONASTER: To suggest that the writer imposes his will on the producer further suggests that we control the production companies, the advertising agencies, and the sponsors. We would like to write about emotion. The writer does not interpret that emotion as violence.

MR. PERIAN: Mr. Knopf, do you have any observations on this subject?

MR. KNOPF: There is a problem today in television which is this: it is an advertising medium. We are in the business to sell a product.

The success or failure of that sale is determined by ratings. A sponsor does not want to offend a potential buyer (or its products).

Therefore it will restrict the writer, the producer, from expressing unpopular truths (which writers want to explore). Therefore you are left with one thing to hold the audience's attention. Sensationalism.

Sensationalism is comprised of sex or violence. We do not (at this time) do sex a lot, so we are left with violence.

MR. PERIAN: Do you feel writers as a group feel powerless, Mr Monaster?

MR. MONASTER: At the moment the writer does not have too great an alternative, short of flatly refusing to work.

MR. PERIAN: Is there nothing else to write about?

MR. MONASTER: I am not as familiar (with this style of writing) as most of my work has been done in the area of situation comedy which is the other extremity of violence. In television you die violently or there is another area in which you die of boredom.

The gallery, especially the press, broke into laughter. Dodd turned to Perian, mouthing "What did he say?" as the laughter grew contagious. Perian cupped a hand over his mouth to conceal his whispered explanation. Dodd didn't like it, didn't like it a bit as the room settled down. I decided to stick my two cents in. Big mistake.

MR. KNOPF: May I make a statement in regard to
                       this, please? I think we must be cautious
                       about condemning all shows. (Especially) in regard to the atmosphere that
                       has been created here today about *Target, The Corrupters*. I happen to think this
                       show has enormous potential. I would
                       not work on it if I did not feel it had the
                       opportunity for content.

MR. PERIAN: Mr. Knopf, now that you have brought
                       this subject up, did you write for *The
                       Corrupters* a story called *The Platinum
                       Highway*?

Oh, shit.

MR. PERIAN: (continuing) I have a memo here from
                       the ABC continuity acceptance editor (Dorothy Brown) on that particular
                       show, on that particular script.

I was not to be interrogated about my participation on *Target, The Corrupters*. It was a condition of our testifying. I stared at Perian, with every dagger my eyes could command. He dropped his to his notes.

MR. PERIAN: (continuing) On page six she admonishes

"Never point a gun directly into the camera and thus into the living rooms of America." Page fifty-one, "This beating is unacceptable as described." Page fifty-six, "This fight is too much." Page seventy-one...

MR. KNOPF: Did you read the script, Mr. Perian?

MR. PERIAN: We have the script. I have not had time to read it.

MR. KNOPF: I would appreciate your reading it and tell me whether you feel that script is excessive violence.

MR. PERIAN: As I said I am referring to...

MR. KNOPF: I would like to comment that often a naked comment such as that can distort a situation, particularly when you do not know what it refers to.

MR. PERIAN: All I am saying is that these descriptions were in the original script, is that correct? Scenes of this type?

MR. KNOPF: Scenes of what type, Mr. Perian? You do not even know what those scenes are.

MR. PERIAN: They have been described by (ABC's continuity acceptance editor) Dorothy Brown.

MR. KNOPF:	No, they have not been described. They have been commented on.
MR. PERIAN:	Is that not sufficient?
MR. KNOPF:	I would leave that to your judgment. I think they are distortions.
MR. PERIAN:	Did you write this script, Mr. Knopf?
MR. KNOPF:	Yes.
MR. PERIAN:	These scenes?
MR. KNOPF:	Yes.
MR. PERIAN:	Did you read Dorothy Brown's commentary?
MR. KNOPF:	Yes.
MR. PERIAN:	Thank you, Mr. Knopf.

In fact what ABC, as *all* networks were suddenly doing, was intensifying their censorship critiques, not so much for us as for the eyes of the Committee.

I looked for Perian in the hall outside the hearing room at the conclusion of the day. I couldn't find him, but Dodd found me, started pumping my hand.

"I think the best hope," he said, "is in the writers. They have the respect of people and the prestige."

I couldn't help wondering what committee he thought he'd been chairing.

Listen, You Son of A Bitch

"Mr. Knopf?"

"Speaking."

"This is Rosemary Clooney."

"Yes, Ms. Clooney."

"So nice to speak to you, Mr. Knopf."

"The pleasure's mine. How can I help you?"

"Well, you know my husband is Jose Ferrer," she said, voice gentle, seductive.

"As I'm well aware," I answered.

"And you're aware, too, that he's a member of the Guild."

"Of course. We're honored to have him."

"Well." It was one of those "wells", the sort that always precedes an obvious conclusion. "He's on assignment, you know, writing a television play."

"I think that's wonderful. Congratulate him for me."

"And, of course," said with an apologetic little laugh, "in the event there's a strike, he'll be allowed to complete the script."

"I'm sorry, Ms. Clooney, but no," I said. "Strike rules call for all writers on assignment, in the event of a strike, to cease and desist from further writing the moment it's called."

There was a pause. "You don't understand," she said, the voice turned gravely. "This is Jose Ferrer."

"No one on assignment will be allowed to continue writing, Ms. Clooney."

I could hear her breathing through the pause. "Listen you son of as bitch..!"

The year was 1966. I'd followed Nate Monaster to the presidency of the Television Branch when he'd been elected overall Guild President of the two combined branches. Now I had the job, President of the Writers Guild of America, West.

The television writers were stalled in negotiations again with Management, the first since 1960, all boiling down to one contentious issue. With all else we'd won in 1960, we'd made one colossal mistake. We'd accepted a royalty plan, a percentage of producer's revenue, as payments for television reruns.

On paper the royalty plan had sounded great. Creative accounting reduced our rerun payments to ridiculous sums on the claims there *were* no profits, some writers receiving checks for as little as a dollar ninety eight for an initial network summer rerun of their work. The only retribution we could come up with, admittedly petulant, was not to cash them, framing them instead to hang on our walls, thereby hoping to foul their bookkeeping. Our negotiating committee, again led by Nate, was demanding the plan be junked, replaced with significant, specified residual payments.

Management was adamant. "No way, no how!"

Another strike seemed imminent. It was the membership's call, but my views were well known. I was resolute about leading a walkout if Management didn't accede to our demands. Thus a "son of a bitch" to Rosemary Clooney.

She wasn't the only one that felt that way. At a strike meeting which I chaired, I was asking members of the Television Branch to vote a strike authorization, giving Guild leadership the power to call a strike as and if it felt necessary, to give the negotiating committee the heft it needed to back our demands. It was *my* turn now to see nothing but teeth. And the challenges from the floor were familiar.

"What guarantees do we have we'll win?"

"How long would we be out?"

"Are we set up for no interest loans to see us through?"

"It's a gaggle of geese, a pride of lions, a worry of writers," screen writer and Broadway playwright Isobel Lennart once said, and she was right.

"There *are* no guarantees," I answered. "You're asking for guarantees that don't exist. But without your strike authorization we have no chance. With it we do."

"He's lying to you! He's lying!"

The shout came from E Jack Neuman. Jack, one of the all time truly superb television writers, was a close friend of mine. We had lunch together. A lot. Jack also liked to tipple. And that night he'd kept the bar open mostly by himself. Nate Monaster, who was developing a play for Broadway that was now on hold, as usual saved the evening.

"You are being asked to fight for a principle: fair payment for reuse of your work, which is your right," Nate told a crowd that was on the edge of turning surly. "Principle isn't principle until it costs. The cost of this is your vote."

We got it, and further, help from a source we never expected. The Screenwriters. A year before it wouldn't have happened.

The Guild election of 1965 had been contentious, not between my opponent and me, but between the Guild's two branches, Television and Screen. Screenwriters had established the Screenwriters Guild decades before, at great effort and under personal threat not to do so from studio heads, and now saw themselves sharing equality with television writers flooding in upon their hard-won domain. They were resentful. Even though the two branches had separate contracts with Management, with separate termination dates, they saw the emphasis of Management-Guild conflicts most generally over television issues, less and less over screen. The up-coming negotiations of 1966 did not affect them, and most had no interest in supporting television writers in their fight.

Jim Poe had run and won the presidency of the Screen Branch largely on an elitist campaign. His screen people wanted as little to do with those of us in television as they could manage. They were joined at the hip by the Guild's amalgamation agreement, but that's as far as they were willing to go. Thus the pot simmered. In the late fall of 1963 it had boiled over.

In March of every year the Guild held its annual Awards Dinner. Usually in the International Ball Room of the Beverly Hilton Hotel, seventeen hundred people, the room's capacity, gathered for the industry's toughest-to-get ticket aside from the Academy Awards. The calling card wasn't the awards themselves. It was the show: skits and musical numbers backed by a live orchestra, wit-tily, often cruelly, lampooning the industry, written by writers, per-formed by top available movie stars. The targets, which were pro-ducers, agents, studio heads, loved it. To be trashed at the Writers Awards Dinner Show was proof of their industry stature.

There were nominations and awards for Original Screenplay. And for Adapted Screen Play. There were service awards, named for screen writers who in the past had sacrificed and worked tire-lessly for the Guild. What there were not were television awards. None. Having been initiated before the amalgamation of the two branches, the Awards Dinner had remained "pure". Screen only, the annual television writers' awards given out, often as not, during a modestly attended television branch annual business meeting. It rankled. All the more so, because the Screen Awards dinner was written more and more by television comedy and sketch writers.

At a monthly Screen and Television Council Meeting in 1963, the Television Writers made it clear and plain. They wanted parity, their awards presented the same night as Screen, at the Guild's annual Awards Dinner and they wanted it starting now.

Ernie Lehman led the outcry against it. In a painfully moving oration he pleaded that Screen be allowed its one final vestige of hallowed territory, immune from the taint of television. The Screen Board went with him. The Television Board revolted. Screen wanted its show to be theirs alone? Let them write it. Television would have a show of its own.

It did, falling into the greatest piece of luck imaginable. Allan Sherman, comedy writer-producer-director, had just created his forever-famous parody, "Hello Mudduh, Hello Faddah," and was now an overnight national star. Stars attract stars. Everyone, it seemed, wanted to be on the show with Allan. Fred MacMurray, Tony Curtis, Polly Bergen, Rock Hudson, Carl Reiner, Jackie Cooper, Phil Silvers, Jane Powell, Jack Benny, Mary Tyler Moore. It was riotous and cutting and a smash hit.

Three weeks later the Screen Branch followed with its show, written solely by Screenwriters. It was a mess. Witless and vulgar. Finger pointing was all over the place. Television writers had proven they were far from second class talents, and for some that went down hard. One man turned it around. Screen Branch President Jim Poe.

Jim was a rascal. Tall, handsome, debonair, with an infectious personality and charm, Jim was known to traffic with some of the town's freewheeling rogues. Drugs and excessive alcohol were rumored to be part of it. Probably more than a rumor as Jim, when I knew him, had turned to Alcoholics Anonymous. But he was also his own man, with the guts to back it up.

John Frankenheimer, Director of *The Manchurian Candidate*, had a reputation of despising writers. No writer I ever talked to enjoyed the experience of working with him, talented though he was. In an interview he'd publicly stated, "Just give me a first draft and I'll get any a-- h--- to fix it." At the following Writers Award Dinner, Jim, in his role as President of the Screen Branch, publicly gave "The Yellow Ream Award" to Frankenheimer, cascading five hundred fluttering blank yellow pages out into the audience. It was uproarious, the crowd ate it up. At seven o'clock the following morning, Frankenheimer, who was not in the audience, was on the phone to Jim. "Any alley, buddy! Any alley!"

For all his initial determination to separate screen from the trials of television, Jim found himself drawn to the television writers' conflict and came to appreciate the dire nature of it. So much so, that on his own, he announced that should television writers strike, no screenwriter would cross their picket lines.

Management's collective heads spun about so fast you could hear bones crack. Exactly what did Jim mean? they wanted to know.

No screenwriter would cross picket lines, Jim repeated.

He was speaking specifically, of course, Management queried, it was about not going through picket lines set up in front of studios, right? That wouldn't count working at home, pages mailed in or picked up by messengers, right?

No screenwriter would cross picket lines!

Again and again Jim repeated his mantra, no specifics as to what exactly he meant. The producers grew restive, then bellicose. They wanted a clear, unadulterated statement of precisely what Jim meant! They had their statement, Jim told them.

No screenwriter would cross picket lines!

One hour before the television contract was to expire, Management gave television writers what they were asking for. The royalty plan was out, residuals were in, specific hard cash payments for reuse of their work.

Nate Monaster went back to his play that would open on Broadway and fold in one night. Hovering over a cup of coffee in Manhattan's Stage Door Deli the following morning, Nate looked up to see Oscar-winning comedy writer, Frank Tarloff sliding onto the chair before him.

"Nate, what's the matter?" Frank asked sympathetically.

"I don't know," Nate replied. "How do I go back and face everybody?"

"Well, you got one thing going for you," Frank said.

"What's that?"

"Think how many of your friends you made happy."

Gray is for Horses, Never the PD

"You miserable Hollywood shit! You Hollywood phony..!"

1967. We were seated in a booth in a Burbank restaurant for lunch, Leonard Freeman, Stuart Whitman and I. CBS had hired me to write a pilot script for a ninety minute series concept, *Cimarron Strip*, now completed and given a go to production. It was to deal with the range war between farmers and cattlemen in 1888 over the last remaining cattleman's refuge in the Oklahoma territory. Mike Dann, senior vice-president of programming at the network, announced he would order filming of the pilot if we got one of three actors to play the lead. Stuart Whitman was one of the choices. He accepted the part.

Stu, who had gone from television to screen where he'd done some exemplary work, was now moving back to the small screen. Watching him at that lunch table I could see he was wary as we sat discussing the casting of supporting roles on the show.

Leonard Freeman, who'd been hired to produce the pilot, led the discussion. Leonard and I hit it off. An outstanding writer-producer, he was as good as there was, experienced, focused, knowledgeable. As we brought up the name of one respected actor after another to join the cast, Stu batted them down. "A star," he said. And again, to another name I mentioned, "Another star."

Leonard sat back. "Stu, level with me. Are you trying to play it safe?"

Stu began to rock, back and forth, his face turning crimson. "You miserable Hollywood..."

Leonard was right. It was exactly what Stu was doing, and I felt for him. He didn't know either one of us. Whether or not he felt he was being thrust into a milieu beneath him, that his movie career was hitting a de-escalation, I don't know. What he didn't know was how close we'd come to having no pilot at all.

Stanley Kallis, my old friend from Four Star, was now a CBS program executive. On his own he'd researched a period of American history he thought fascinating -- the cattlemen-held open rangeland across the Cimarron River in the Oklahoma territory that was coveted by farmers, moving west with their families. A wily, seasoned U.S. Marshal, to be played by Whitman, was sent in to keep the lid on, if he could. Thus the series concept.

Stanley's presentation was wonderful, well researched and detailed. He took it to Perry Lafferty, west coast head of CBS, who liked it, ordered a pilot script, asked Stanley whom he wanted to write it. Stanley named me. Perry said fine.

I'd been working on an idea that would eventually take me back into features, but Stanley was impossible to resist. First he had one of the best story minds I knew, and we thought alike. A lot. Second, I saw something unique in his concept. This was not your typical western, your bank robber or outlaw gang being hunted down and brought to justice. It was an opportunity to plumb human motives, feelings and failings, my old themes, as well as people, some decent, some not, caught up in their fight for their past or tomorrow.

Putting my feature on hold, I finished the script, turned it in to high praise from Perry, and dismissive condemnation from a CBS program executive in New York. A negative vote, particularly coming from the east, could be fatal. Perry told Stanley to get to New York and fight for it.

While waiting for Stanley's return with a go or pass on my script, Bette and I threw a party. Gene and Eileen Roddenberry were invited. So were Sam and Hilda Rolfe, and Bruce and Jeannette Geller, along with Frank Cooper, my agent, and his wife Sylvia. I also invited Dad, coming alone, Mother being out of town. It was a night to remember.

Returned from Burgenstock, they'd sold the house in the Palisades, moved into a single story, two bedroom home in Mandeville Canyon, now living on the moderate income off an inheritance Mother received from her parents, along with royalties from the sales of her cookbooks.

From the moment Dad got out of the taxi and entered my house I knew there was going to be trouble. Bruce, Gene and Sam, currently producers, writers and creators of three of the most successful shows on television, *Mission Impossible, Star Trek*, and *Have Gun Will Travel*, were more than Dad could handle. By the end of his third double scotch and two glasses of wine he was loaded for bear. With snide, judgmental comments directed at whomever had the floor, he lacerated Sylvia Cooper who'd made a simple comment with, "What makes you think you're qualified to have an opinion?" Sam Rolfe was ready to hit him, not a good prospect, Sam having been an undefeated heavyweight boxer during his time in the Army. Pushing himself from the table, Dad staggered through the living room to the toilet. I intercepted him as he reemerged.

"Dad, you're ruining my party.'

"Well, if I'm ruining your party, I'll leave."

"I wish you would."

Ordering a cab, I stood with him, both of us silent, at the edge of the driveway awaiting the cab's arrival. His face was stone as he looked off into the night. For the first time I felt for him, felt deeply. He seemed so diminished. The business had passed him by and here were these three young Turks, already internationally acclaimed, and more importantly, I realized, I myself, had risen to the industry's coveted "A" list. He couldn't handle it, because he hadn't designed it. I wasn't his creation. I had achieved my own success on my own which he'd so wanted to be a reflection of himself. And it wasn't. The taxi arrived, he climbed in and left.

The following morning he called. "I just want to tell you," he said, his voice up and cheerful as though nothing had happened at all, "what a wonderful time I had last night."

Two days later Stan Kallis returned from New York. He'd done his job. The pilot was ordered.

I was to be Executive Producer, which was in my contract, but Leonard Freeman became the engine that drove the production. Don Medford, who'd understandably walked off that Dick Powell show I'd written due to Aaron Spelling's lack of attention, was brought on to direct. Still, then as later, Leonard was the guiding force of the show and its savior. The pilot was brought in on time, the dailies looked great, the acting and direction strong. When unexpectedly, a problem. A near fatal one.

Network scheduling for the new season was coming up fast. We had seven days, seven, to assemble a ninety minute show and turn it over to post production for network notes, reediting, color correction, music, looping, sound. As the director, Don Medford had the first cut. He spent the first three days, three of the allotted seven, on the first thirty seconds of the film.

The opening of the show had six cowboys alongside a railroad track, one with his ear to a rail, awaiting the approach of a train bringing farmers into the territory, preparing to ransack it. Don decided to open with what he called "a metric cut," which meant thirty-two frames, then sixteen, eight, four, two, one, followed by a hard cut to the train itself.

There's an old expression in film editing. You can't cut the film you wish you'd shot. And Don hadn't shot it that way. Try as he would he couldn't make it happen. But try he kept on doing, till Leonard, running out of time, took the film away from him.

Don was livid, but the network backed Leonard and so did I. Over four days, ninety six hours, working around the clock with multiple editors, sleep being no option, led by Leonard, we assembled the show. To Don's credit, he'd given us wonderful footage to work with. He was called in to see the result.

The three of us sat in a projection room, watching, Don, Leonard and I. It was a nightmare. Don was a spectacle. Thrashing his body around, he'd impatiently snap his fingers at his intense displeasure at what he was seeing. "Come on, move it! Move! Move! Shit!"

When it was over and the lights came up Don raged at Leonard. It was slow! It lacked continuity, concept, coherence! By any measure, a piece of crap!

I blew. I don't recall ever doing such a thing before or since. Not like that. I was out of my chair in total fury. First, Leonard had heart disease, and everyone knew it, including Don. As such Don was a goddamn bully, attacking a man who didn't dare attack back.

And I said so. I also made clear that Don, screwing around with his undoable metric cut, had nearly put us out of business, saved only by Leonard's dogged, tireless four days of work. If anything was crap, it was Don.

Leonard tried to turn down the heat. He did it with one of the best cutting lines I ever heard. "Don," he said, "this is the first and last time you and I are going to make a film together. Let's make it a good one."

I don't even know if Don heard him. Shaken by my outburst — we'd been friends throughout our time at Four Star — Don stormed from the room. When he was gone Leonard turned to me with words equal in meaning to any awards I'd achieved.

"I wasn't sure. You're a stand up guy."

Thankfully there was a coda to this episode, and it was a good one. The pilot completed, scored by Maurice Jarre who'd written the music for *Lawrence Of Arabia* and *Dr Zhivago*, it made the CBS fall schedule. Don was called in to see the final product, which he did, in a projection room, watching it alone.

I was seated across the parking area getting my shoes shined when Don emerged. He approached me slowly, hands dug into his hip pockets. He reached me, toed the concrete a moment, looked up.

"How could I have been so wrong?"

"You got to tell Leonard."

He did.

Leonard had put aside a project of his own he was developing for CBS when asked to produce the pilot of *Cimarron Strip*. I went to him, asked if he'd stay with the show, at least the first year. I'd give up my Executive Producer title to him, and work with the writers as Supervising Producer.

Leonard thanked me, told me, no. He had his own series to do. I suggested maybe he could put it off for a time, do it later.

He looked at me with a smile, and I knew what he was going to say before he said it.

"I don't view time the same way you do."

He completed his pilot which was shot and made the schedule in the fall of 1968. *Hawaii Five-O* would last twelve years, through 1980. It would receive two Emmys and three more nominations. Leonard never saw the end of it. He died, January 20, 1974, during open-heart surgery.

Stanley Kallis asked CBS for a Created By credit on *Cimarron Strip*, which he richly deserved and I supported, settling myself for a "Developed By" credit. It had been his concept, his presentation, his fight for it in New York. There would have been no *Cimarron Strip* without him. Because he was a CBS executive, the network refused. Stanley left to produce and help guide to prominence a series for Bruce Geller at Desilu Studios. It was *Mission Impossible*.

Cimarron Strip, wholly owned and financed by CBS, was given a favorable time slot. But there were rumors. Perry Lafferty loved the show, and the direction it promised to take. Mike Dann wasn't so sure. *Gunsmoke* had been the western flagship series for CBS for years, and that's what Dann wanted.

A luncheon was called with Perry, Dann and me, at the Polo Lounge in the Beverly Hills Hotel. I rose as Dann arrived, offered my hand in greeting. I'd never met him personally, and this was the first and last time that I would. He took my hand. Sort of. It was like a limp rag, all the while speaking to Perry, ignoring me entirely.

"I think," Dann said finally, after preliminary discussions with Perry were concluded and we'd gotten through the obligatory introductions, "the audience wants the bad fellow do something evil and the good fellow to bring him to justice."

I looked at Perry who was suddenly preoccupied with the olive in his martini.

"Mike," I offered, "I think what you're saying is . . . ."

It's as far as I got. Dann had turned again to Perry. "Now, about Sam Rolfe's pilot."

In the parking lot I bearded Perry. "It's not what he bought," I told him.

Perry had as tough a job as there was at the network. A producer, writer, director, actor, twice nominated for Emmys, his sympathies were with the talent, whom he supported when and as he could. He was also answerable to management, and management was Mike Dann. He tried to thread the needle.

"Give him one in three. Just that. Every third one. The rest your way," he told me.

We tried to. Sort of. Well, not really. And we mostly got away with it through the summer leading up to the fall schedule. First, we were bringing aboard some of the best freelance writers available, coming up with wonderful, well executed concepts. Harlan Ellison, four times Writers Guild Award Winner, placing London's Jack The Ripper in Cimarron City, who totally closes up the town, city violence overwhelming western violence. William Wood, off *Kraft Playhouse* and *Chrysler Theater*, writing about an old Indian fighter, a seasoned professional soldier played by Richard Boone, who can't give up war, though there's no war left to fight unless he manufactures one. Richard Fielder, Jack Curtis, Hal Sitowitz, Harold Swanton, the latter of *Alfred Hitchcock Presents* and *Goodyear Theater*, accurately portraying Wyatt Earp as a product of his own invention, arriving in Cimarron to add to his legend, creating anarchy and then "heroically" setting about to resolve it. Mike Dann had cats when he saw that one. Earp was a national legend, falsely earned or not. It would be too confusing to his audience to show his duplicity and connivance. He made us loop every reference to Wyatt Earp with Wiley Harp.

Still we plunged ahead, overwhelming Dann's distrust with not only the level of writers we were hiring, but actors as well. Beau Bridges, Robert Duvall, Richard Boone, Joseph Cotton, Tuesday Weld, Broderick Crawford, Suzanne Pleshette, Tom Skeritt, Jon Voight.

The scripts were good to outstanding, so were the shows. And then in September we went on the air, and all of Dann's misgivings seemed justified. Our ratings were barely fair, remaining that way through winter.

Stu was becoming agitated, demanded an accounting. Were we going a second year or not? A meeting was set up to take place in a suite at the Beverly Hills Hotel with Perry Lafferty, but first, we'd meet for dinner, Stu and I and his William Morris agent, Hal Ross.

Hal was an old friend, one of the best in the agency business for handling and calming edgy clients. It was determined Hal and I would meet first at a Sunset Strip restaurant in West Hollywood, ahead of Stu who would join us at the conclusion of the day's shooting. Putting our heads together Hal and I agreed we would have a quiet dinner, get into nothing contentious, settle Stu down prior to the Lafferty meeting.

Shortly, Stu arrived, but came from the set still in costume, black Western clothes, black boots, black hat. Spotting us he started toward our table when Don Rickles, in a voice you could hear to Burbank, boomed out, "Hey! Big movie star! Doin' TV!" It was the end of the night, even when Perry later promised "An 18 share! That's all it's going to take to stay on the air. An 18 share!" An 18 share? If you didn't get 20 you were toast.

I was in the midst of developing a script with Sy Salkowitz when it all came to a head. At least, for me. A well respected writer off *Naked City*, Sy had brought in an idea I loved. A freewheeling cavalry veteran clashes with his hard ass, rigid, by the book Sergeant Major, over what appears to be nothing more than a frivolous event. Given a choice of resigning or facing court martial, the soldier resigns, rounds up some soldier friends, kidnaps the Sergeant Major and puts him on a kangaroo court martial of his own. During the trial it's realized the Sergeant Major was right, the soldier was wrong, that the Sergeant Major was responsible for saving lives caused by the careless, supposedly trivial behavior of the soldier. It was a story in which the heavy turns out to be the hero. Mike Dann hated it, it wasn't a Western, would only confuse his audience with its turnabout. He told me, through Perry, to get rid of the writer. I asked Perry what would happen if I didn't. Perry, anticipating Dann's reaction, warned me, "Better him than you."

The writer, Sy Salkowitz, was a close friend of mine. Our kids romped together on the sand at Sy's beach house. We figuratively held each other's hand through our divorces. And something else. My long time complexity, cowardice vs courage, was no longer just a theme to be written about, it was at hand. What was it Nate Monaster had said? "Principal isn't principal until it costs?" I told Perry I was sorry, I couldn't get rid of the writer.

Cleaning out my office I left a note for my replacement:

> Ambivalent heavies
> Are hereby forbid.
> Grey is for horses,
> Never the Id.

You'd think that was the end of it. No such luck. My eleven-year-old daughter, Susan, got a call from a research polling company, asking what her favorite show was. She had no doubt.

"The Monkees."

President of Hollywood

Leigh Vance and I were seated together on a half full Russian Aeroflot, flying the American and English contingent to Moscow for the first conference of the International Writers Guild, a loose confederation of screen and television writers from Europe, the U.S., Canada, Australia, New Zealand and Israel, among others. The sun was setting behind us as we flew east from London.

Leigh, an English writer who'd migrated to a successful career in the U.S. was holding forth, explaining how he'd become a vegetarian. A Spitfire fighter pilot during the Battle of Britain, he'd claimed to be a vegetarian because the food for vegetarians was far better than what was being offered the rest in the squadron mess hall. Surviving one combat mission after another against the Luftwaffe, it became a mystical survival calling that stayed with him. While in London, Leigh took me to the pub his squadron had frequented during the war. On the wall were framed photographs of the pilots, one and all, gold frames encasing those who'd been killed. Two thirds were in gold frames.

Suddenly Leigh wasn't talking. He was staring out the window. Something was wrong. We were heading *toward* the sun instead of *away* from it! We were flying west! A question to the stewardess got nothing, only "Nyet, nyet!" as she moved forward, disappearing into the pilot's compartment.

A look out the window showed we were going down, way down, no city below us, so low now we were skimming the tops of pine trees.

It had all begun a year earlier.

In 1936 Joseph Stalin commissioned Aleksei Yakovlevich Kapler to write a screenplay on Lenin. Kapler was a Jew, and Stalin hated Jews, but Kapler was also Russia's leading screenwriter. During the process, Stalin's thirteen year old daughter fell in love with Kapler, handsome and twenty-six years older. Infuriated, Stalin imprisoned Kapler in a labor camp.

By the late 1960s Stalin was dead, and Kapler, long since released, was once again Russia's leading screenwriter, anxious to establish relationships with his western counterparts. Thus was the Writers Guild Foundation formed for the initial purpose of soliciting private donations to bring Kapler and his fellow Soviet writers to Hollywood to meet our members. As founder of the Foundation, Jim Webb, along with Mel Shavelson, and to a lesser extent I, then National Chairman of the Writers Guild of America, East and West, were among the hosts. Dinners were held in homes after all day meetings at the Guild where we found the Russians remarkably open, giving the impression they wanted to bring their government kicking and screaming into the twentieth century.

A year later Kapler reciprocated, helping to form the IWG, its first convention to be held in Moscow. It wasn't an easy thing for Kapler to accomplish considering east-west tensions. Our own State Department sent out a pamphlet of cautions and warnings to those of us slated to represent the U.S. Among them? Assume we were being monitored, watched and listened to wherever we went, our hotel rooms included. Further, we were warned, resist temptation. Indonesian President Sukarno apparently hadn't. Brought in by the KGB, hoping to gain top secret information from him, they showed him film of his exploits with a Russian prostitute. To his credit, he's reported to have applauded loudly, proclaiming, "My finest performance! My finest performance!"

Nothing fights harder for its existence than paranoia. Later, when I told Mel Shavelson I'd searched my room in the Rossiya Hotel where we were quartered and could find no hidden mikes, he told me, "What makes you think when you hang up the phone is disconnected."

Travelling first to London to meet with the British writers, I was luxuriating in my six foot tub at the Connaught Hotel, just divorced, wondering where my private life would go from there, when the bathroom door burst open, and in came the night manager and two police, guns drawn.

"Sorry, sir, second story man," I was told. And out the bathroom window they went onto the roof.

But now we were in that Aeroflot Ilyushin, heading down. Bracing for God knows what, we were all at once over a tarmac, the plane landing at an obscure isolated field, nobody knowing where we were. Ushered into a small terminal, we discovered we were in Sweden. Nobody would tell us why, when suddenly another Aeroflot flew in, on its way to Moscow from Belgium, also half-full, with the rest of our group. The two flights were combined into one. Russian enterprise. Why send in two half-full planes?

Arriving in Moscow after midnight, we deplaned through a narrow cordon of heavily armed soldiers, entered to find ourselves individually locked in tiny cubicles, facing stone-faced uniformed customs officers searching to see if our names were to be found in a book the size of the New York phone directory. Passports stamped, we were unlocked, passed through into the deserted terminal where our Russian guide, a jolly fellow with glasses as thick as the bottoms of Coke bottles, greeted us in broken English.

"Is welcome. Is everybody to get on bus."

As we searched for our off-loaded bags Sam Zebba, one of two Israeli writers, came up to me, asked if everyone had been given back their passports. I told him they had. He hadn't. Nor had his fellow Israeli. Everyone else had their passports returned but these two.

People were starting to work their way toward the doors leading out to waiting busses. I told everyone to hold it, wait. I went to our guide, explained we all had our passports except the Israelis.

"Is no problem," he told me. "Is everyone onto bus."

I told him, no, it *was* a problem. It was a time of major discord between Russia and Israel. There was no diplomatic accord between the two countries. These two Israeli writers were not going to be held hostage to it. No one was leaving the terminal till they had their passports in hand.

He blanched, quickly crossed the terminal to a door and went through it. Among our group was a Norwegian writer, with him his girlfriend, gorgeous, an actress. Stamping her foot in pique she declared she was tired and hungry, and was getting onto that bus! When I told her what the hold up was about, she immediately backed off, apologized, joined the sentiment of the others, which was unanimous.

Our jovial guide returned with a look on his face that said all was resolved. "Is no problem," he said. "Is passports back at hotel in morning. Is everybody onto bus."

No, I said. I was sorry. No one was leaving the terminal until everyone had their passports.

Across the terminal, by the door, sat a man in a brown suit working on papers at a small desk. Beside him stood a soldier armed with what I supposed was an AK-47. Crossing to him I repeated my position, no one was leaving till all had their passports. He stared at me, or through me, saying nothing. If he understood a word I said he gave no indication of it. I returned to the group feeling stupid from what probably appeared to be grandstanding, but no one criticized. Neither did anyone insist upon leaving. It was a sit down strike and it gained results. At three in the morning, three hours after our arrival, the Israelis' passports miraculously appeared and were returned.

"Is nothing political," our Guide assured us as we headed for the busses.

The following day our Norwegian actress showed her remorse at her behavior by going to a Moscow synagogue. Sam Zebba who accompanied her said the men were so enthralled by her appearance they couldn't help themselves, they swarmed her, hands going everywhere. As she later confirmed, "Everywhere!"

The Rossiya Hotel was Moscow's newest and largest, six stories, six thousand beds, located in back of St Basils, between Red Square and the Moscow River. It had twelve elevators. Three were operating. You got your room key from a woman seated at a desk on your floor, giving her a sight line left and right to anyone entering any room. Meetings, led by Jim Webb, voted head of the International Writers Guild, were held at an immense table in an equally immense room. Headphones were worn, affording translations into various languages. The meetings, as I recall them, were mostly boring, due to a predominance of discussions on copyright, largely and endlessly conducted by French lawyers who were loathe to give up their microphones.

Copyright was and remains a sore subject for American film and television writers, having long ago given it over to our employers. In fact there is hardly a writer's contract drawn that does not make the network or studio "author" of our material. Others may remember the conference differently, I remember it as one long drawn out drone.

The Russian writers, however, were terrific hosts, and our socialization, conversations and burgeoning friendships with them turned out to be the ultimate achievement of the trip that made it so worth while. The cliché about Russians and alcohol, however, is a cliché for good reason. Mike Blankfort and I were entertained one day at a luncheon by two of our counterparts. A bottle of brandy and a bottle of vodka were placed on our table. Mike and I each had one glass of brandy. Both bottles were empty at the end of the meal.

Alcohol proved heavy duty in Moscow. It was everywhere, and there were consequences. More than once we saw people run into the street to pull a fall down drunk from the gutter and hurry him into a building out of sight. We witnessed the reason. If the police got to him first, they'd openly, publicly beat him as an example.

Other than that our stay was festive. There was a gala on the Fourth of July at the American Embassy, a Russian circus, a ballet, a luncheon at a sky high circular restaurant.

"Is no pictures, please," we were told.

There was a meal with Kapler at a luxurious restaurant,

"Don't worry about Kapler," I was told when questioning the cost to him of the dinner.

We had taxis and transportation available to us at request, visits to the Kremlin, it's museums filled with ermine cloaks worn by the Czars.

"Why display this?" I asked an interpreter.

"To show what the people revolted against," she explained.

Then, the night after the conference ended, everything stopped. No taxis. No transportation. Leigh Vance was flying on to Leningrad with Jim and Sue Webb. Jim was sick, the beginning of cancer, and Leigh made it clear to the hotel not only did they have to leave early the next morning to get to the airport, but Jim had to have something to eat before leaving.

"Is no problem," Leigh was told, "Is food in restaurant."

Morning came, the restaurant wasn't open, wouldn't be for another hour.

"Is no problem, food at airport."

Arriving at the airport, Leigh approached the courtesy desk, asked where food was being served.

"Is no food."

"This man must eat, he's sick," Leigh explained.

"No food."

"You don't understand. Very important man. President of Hollywood."

"Oooh. President of *Hollywood*?" Out came the food.

It wasn't the only nail-biting exodus from Moscow. There was mine.

The morning following our arrival, we were gathered in the hotel dining room for breakfast. Across from me as I was dining on a flat egg pancake (no matter what you ordered it was always a flat egg pancake) sat an Australian engineer with a plane to catch for home. Beside him was his Russian interpreter from the Institute of Languages, willowy, attractive, long-haired, late twenties, her body cat-like beneath a sheer patterned dress.

"Have you been assigned an interpreter?" she asked.

I look around to see whom she was talking to. She was talking to me.

"Let me see him to a taxi, I'll be right back," as she led the Aussie toward the street.

Her name was Maria, and for the next six days we played a game of flirtation and innuendo in our free time away from the conference, in and out of museums, tea rooms and department stores that had much on display, but nothing for sale.

It was our final night in Moscow, everyone gathered in the cavernous lobby of the hotel, saying our farewells, flights to catch in the morning, mine a British Airways at ten to London, when Maria was at my side.

"I have a girl friend who has an apartment. She's out of town." Years later I would be found to have tachycardia, excessive heart beat. That's when it started. "You won't be disappointed," she added.

Three busses and two hours later Maria was leading me up a third floor walkup and into a single one room apartment. A hutch, containing everything of value to its owner, was all that separated the sleeping quarters from what served as a tiny living room area. There was an alcove with a hot plate, and a dank, floor patched bathroom, no hot water. The rules in Moscow? If you wanted to trade up you had to find someone willing to trade down.

We weren't there for lessons in real-estate, which Maria quickly made clear. Giving myself the best of it, it was not my finest hour.

Let me rephrase that. My finest five minutes. It was well after midnight. I was two hours from the hotel which was God knows where, in forbidding surroundings, a plane to catch in nine hours. I was slipping into my pants when I heard the most chilling nine words of my life.

"You going to run out on me, big boy?"

The blood can run cold. It's true. And then it turned hot as one name came to mind. Sukarno! Idiot! I'd been warned, and there I was, lured by a Russian siren into a trap, God knows how many cameras on me, the KGB about to burst into the room.

What did I have to tell them? There had to be something to be set up like this! What did I know that they'd want to know? It ran through my head like the speed of light. I'd been in the Air Corps, the finance department! Did they want to know about payrolls? I'd been to the White House, to a presidential signing in the Rose Garden. Did they want to know the layout? I knew writers from Hungary, Romania, Russia! Courage swelled within me. I'd tell them nothing! Nothing! If it meant going to a gulag..!

When it all came down with a thud. Maria had dressed, was at the door, waiting for us to leave. The three busses back to the hotel were in silence. I knew I'd have to face her in the morning at breakfast, which I delayed as long as possible. She was already at the table when I came in, friendly and smiling as though nothing had gone wrong at all, which I took to be a way of saving my face. When I realized. A contingent of businessmen had just arrived from Dublin, and across from her sat this attractive red haired Irishman.

"Have you been assigned an interpreter?" she asked him. He answered he hadn't. "Let me see the American to his taxi. I'll be right back."

As for the rest of my memory of my week in Russia, the people were great. Walk down Gorky Street at eleven o'clock at night, you'd think you were in Milwaukee. The young were out, hand in hand. The Russians I met, especially the youthful interpreters, Maria included, seemed to love Americans, desperately wanted to visit the U.S. Could I please, please send them some books. Steinbeck, Mark Twain, and anything on Jack Kennedy. Once home, I did so, sent off a dozen. Follow up communication revealed they never got past Russian customs.

Emperor of the North Pole

"Barring accidents, a good hobo, with youth and agility, can hold a train down despite all the efforts of the train-crew to ditch him."

Walter Newman was in my office above Manny Dwork's tailor shop, reclaimed since leaving Four Star. A small, worn blue-backed book was in his hand, *The Road*, by Jack London, opened to a chapter entitled *Holding Her Down*. Published in 1906, the pages were nearing their end, yellow-brown, wafer thin.

"There's a movie in this," Walter said, handing it to me.

I read it. In public domain, there was nothing of a story in the book that I could see. But that one chapter, dealing with the near-death dangers, the sheer physical acts of confrontation, hobo vs train-crew, were incredible, though where to go with it I hadn't a clue, knowing little or nothing of either.

Taking myself to the north campus research library at UCLA, I was stunned at what I found: a whole shelf of books detailing hobo lore from 1880 through the great depression, their camps on the edge of railway junctions, their unique means of communication atop water towers, their techniques of survival, imaginative names. There were accounts of their battles with railroad cops and among themselves over ownership of preteen runaways used and trained for begging. I found tales of road kids, running in packs, as dangerous and vicious as piranhas. I read of their heroes, "bo's," who could tackle any "death" train and ride it, taking on the railroad's freight conductors, known as "shacks," who had their own reputations to preserve that nobody rode their trains without a ticket.

As I read through two dozen books, a concept for a movie began to evolve. It would be set during the mid-1930s depression, when riding the rails was a way of life for desperate men. A run up Oregon's Willamette Valley. It was colorful and offered opportunity. Woods, freight yards, junctions, farmland, towns, the river. The lead character would be a hobo named A-No.1 (there'd been one in the 1890s with such a name), who'd anoint himself "Emperor Of The North Pole" in a typical flight of self-aggrandizement, but a legend among the grizzled tramps congregating among the camps along the rail line, who would take on an infamous "Shack", a sadistic conductor willing to do whatever was necessary to keep freeloaders off his decrepit four car freight train.

That, however, was a situation, an event. It wasn't a story. I'd long since put my early preoccupation with cowardice and courage behind me. I was now preoccupied with the environment within which I was working. One thing that rankled was the myth, all too serviced in Hollywood, that one had to be famous, important, renowned, on somebody's "A" list to be worthy of note.

Thematically, perhaps allegorically, I had it. Two men in a little known or cared about world, but their world, all they knew, fighting it out for supremacy as potent and charged as Louis vs Schmeling were on a world stage.

Still, what was the story? I knew it would have to come from A-No.1. He was the driving force of the play, the hero. I looked back at my work. I'd written a lot about heroes. Perversely or otherwise, I'd usually given them an Achilles heel, a vulnerability, hidden though it was, that would or could be their undoing. What would that be for A-No.l? He was a loner as these top train riding hoboes were, capable of violence and surviving violence, cunning, crafty, wary of human contact, knowing that could take him down, thereby invulnerable to human relationships. I felt I was heading into an unsolvable dead end.   Then I ran into Cigaret. Given to some road kid of earlier days, I loved the name. Suppose, the battle joined with the Shack, a young punk, a novice, full of false bravado and bluster, out to make a name for himself, horns in on the action.

CIGARET

I got my name written on towers from Seattle to Mobile! I been where it's mean and I want it that way. I ain't tryin' to scare you. When I get hold of that Shack, I'm goin' to bust his ass bad.

Suppose, against his better judgment, A-No.1 rescues the kid, takes him under his wing, their relationship in part adversarial as the weary elder eventually tries to educate the young fool how to survive on Shack's train.

A-NO.1

You're a tramp, a dead beat. Where do you think you're at? Damn, boy, you ain't even ready for a half grown girl. One of those Los Angeles women get hold of you and you'll cry for your Mama. Get your head up. I'll tell you once. You got a chance to be a good bum.

Looming, as the train plows up Oregon's Willamette Valley toward Portland, is the "Shack", out to do his job at any cost, humiliated that A-No.1 has ridden his train at all.

SHACK   I'm not giving away another free ride! He wants to try and deck that, he'll end up selling pencils!

Suppose the kid, once thinking he's learned the ways of the road from A-No.1, decides to betray him, to take his place.

CIGARET   Drag your ass back to the Jesus Shouters and tell 'em they got a stew bum for the choir. This bo's headin' out, he's on his way. And that ain't just to look around. I'm going to parade, high monkey-monk of everything. Emperor of the North Pole! Slashin' right and left with my razor, puttin' my fist into more faces'n you can figger. I'm talkin' straight, you better listen. I ain't stickin' with you anymore.

I had my story. Except. Why would A-No.1 allow this kid along on his ride, pulling him out of one disaster after another, violating his own credo that "I don't give lessons, I don't take students!" Ego? The bone weary loneliness that eventually comes with being the "Emperor"?

I liked what I had and hadn't the vaguest idea how to get it into development, until I met Peter Bart. You don't make things happen alone in this business, at least I never did. In my professional life to this point there'd been Millard Kaufman, Vince Fennelly, Dick Powell, Stanley Kallis, Perry Lafferty, Leonard Freeman, and yes, my Father. Now there was Peter Bart.

Peter, who'd later become Editor In Chief of Daily Variety, was then vice-president in charge of production at Paramount Studios under Robert Evans. I'd met Peter socially, had been to his home, played paddle tennis at his beach club, barefoot, blistering my feet. He invited me to lunch at Paramount, no agenda, strictly casual, asked in passing what I was up to. I ran the *Emperor Of The North Pole* concept past him, mostly to learn if he had any ideas where I might go with the thing.

"Any interest in doing it here?" he asked?

I was given an office and a secretary, Rose Serber, whose time card I had to sign daily. Taking a page from Charley Lederer, I did so, perversely penning it with such as "Henry The Eighth," "Richard Nixon," "Joe Namath," even Charley's renowned "Peter Rabbit." Nobody ever said a word.

"I'm not going to let some director screw this up," Peter said protectively when I turned in the script months later. To my delight, he put me together with Marty Ritt.

Oscar-nominated for *Hud* starring Paul Newman, Marty had just come off directing *The Molly Maguires* for Paramount, a solid choice, in my eyes, for my project. Paid a large fee for working with me on revisions with no guarantee of a film commitment till Paramount saw the final pages, we met at Marty's house. Once. In the Huntington Palisades. His first pronouncement, cheerfully offered, was the only thing he liked about the script was the names. His second pronouncement—there was no second pronouncement. What there was were a pressing series of phone calls as Marty tried to find a gift he'd had in mind for Paul Newman, clearly wanting to maintain the relationship he'd begun with the megastar on *Hud*.

Seasoned to this sort of thing years before by Phil Yordan, I rode out the meeting, Marty apologizing, promising we'd pick it up after the weekend.

It never happened. What Paramount learned was that Marty was doing the same thing all around town, taking holding fees on various other projects, not just mine. Bob Evans and Peter Bart apparently took umbrage, pulled the project from Marty. Which was fine. Except there was no one to replace him.

My deal with the studio was peculiar. At least to me. Paramount would have the property for two years. Then I would have it for two years in what was called turnaround, with the understanding that if I could move it somewhere else, I would first have to reimburse Paramount for all charges accrued against the project. Which would include, but not be limited to, my deal for writing the script, secretarial fees, Xeroxing, office expenditures, phone and messenger costs. At which time, after my two years, the project would revert to Paramount for another two years, then back to me, so on and so forth. Still there was nothing precluding me from trying to put it together while still under Paramount's aegis.

Scripts can get hot, then cold just as fast, and mine was clearly headed for the freezer. I got it to Kirk Douglas. He liked it, couldn't make it happen. I sent it to George Seaton, two Oscars, three nominations. I'd known George since I was a kid, and that was the problem. He just couldn't do it, he said. Too physical, he was too old. On a whim I sent it to Sam Peckinpah.

The phone rang two days later. "Get your ass over here!" Sam said. "We're doing this damn thing!"

Why hadn't I thought of Sam earlier? He was perfect for it,

would be the first to understand the lead character. Given his pro-clivity for going it alone, doing it his way, contrary, ornery—hell, he *was* A-No.1, and one of the few writer-directors I knew if he were to tell me, "I'm making some changes," I'd have said, "Go for it!"

I met Sam in his office at Warner Brothers. There were skis leaning in one corner, shirts and underwear on book shelves, pants hanging from a light fixture. The man was *living* there.

This was Sam's kind of show. As I hoped, he nderstood it per-fectly. He wasn't interested in talking about changes for the moment, only where he could shoot it, how he'd cast it, how Warners would buy it for him away from Paramount and do it there, where he had a house-keeping deal, meaning an office and secretary, and, should he bring something in, he and the studio would sit down and talk.

I left on a high, only to be brought crashing down a week later. Sam had his problems with Warner Brothers. Whatever they were I was never to find out, but they would not pay him what he wanted to direct this or any other film, and possibly neither would any one else. There were rumors Sam had burned bridges around town, that he was an incredible but out-of-control talent few could trust. I can't vouch for that, I never saw it. I always liked Sam. Others didn't, didn't get along with him, found him irascible and offensive. I never saw that either. Twice we came close to working together, and twice it didn't happen. How I wish it had.

As for *Emperor Of The North Pole*, it was now in the freezer, shoved to the back, lying frozen, forgotten. Paramount's two years were up, and my two nearly so, no more action, not even a nibble.

I'd put it behind me, gone on to other things, among them a pi-lot for Universal starring George Peppard which was shot but not scheduled. I liked George. I found him extraordinarily straightforward and honest, as he came into my office one day, asked if we could talk about a scene. He closed the door and sat down.

"What's the problem?" I asked.

"I'm not great at sensitivity."

The scene was between a father and his long unseen young son. Some actors will pounce on something they can't accomplish with, "This is crap!" Or, "This isn't dialogue!" Or they'll do it and butcher it. George didn't. It took guts, and a very secure actor, to do what he did. I liked the scene as written, but if it was wrong for George, it was wrong for the show. I thanked him for telling me, told him, "Let's fix it." We did, working together till he was comfortable. A different scene, but it worked. Hold fast to your precious creations, you can do so for a price you might not want to pay.

There was a Movie Of The Week, a two-man show with Eli Wallach and Robert Culp for ABC, and the usual run of pilot projects, and then a phone call from my agent, Bob Eisenbach.

"Be on notice," Bob told me, "Paramount wants to buy out your interest in *Emperor*."

It made no sense. There were six weeks to go before it reverted to them for another two years. Something was going on. We decided to sweat it, told Paramount, no. We quickly found out what was happening.

Robert Aldrich, director of the brilliant World War II film *Attack*, along with later works, *Flight Of The Phoenix* and *The Dirty Dozen*, had been courted by Paramount, given its library of unfilmed scripts to consider. Shaking the ice from mine he read it, announced it was the one he wanted to make.

How and why Bob got it away from Paramount and took it to Fox I, per usual, was never to learn, but that's what he did. Bringing aboard Lee Marvin as A-No.1, Ernie Borgnine as Shack, Bob's script notes were minimal, such as:

"I don't mind killing an actor, I just want to know why?"

Only one major change was called for. I'd ended my script with a brutal fight between A-No.1 and Shack in which the hobo gives himself up, taking himself and Shack off the train, saving Cigaret, leaving the shallow punk atop the caboose as the train plows on, with the sickening realization that he's now the "Emperor," and all that entails.

"Lee Marvin will never give himself up for that kid," Bob told me.

The new ending? Shack has cornered Cigaret, is closing in on him, stalking him across the top of moving freight cars, sledge hammer in hand.

SHACK   Oh, you can keep runnin', kid. But
                         you're runnin' out of train.

When A-No.1 intervenes, takes on Shack in their brutal fight, ending with A-No.1 throwing Shack off his train. Cigaret, full of mouth, chortles away with relief and the thrill of victory as he approaches A-No.1.

CIGARET   Me and you, if we ain't a team! We'll go
                         to prison and free the prisoners! We'll
                         capture Mexico! Do in Rome as the Da-
                         goes do, knock down everything we see,
                         all stuck on ourselves! Cigaret and A-
                         No.1!

At which A-No.1 lifts the punk off his feet and pitches him from the moving train into the river, shouts after him as the train steams away.

| A-NO.1 | Try the barns, kid! Run like the devil, find an empty! Get a can and take up mooching! Tackle back doors for a nickel! Tell your story, make their eyes run! Only stay off the rails, give it up! It's a bum world for a bum! |

Bob Aldrich was right, turning it from being an unfulfilling tragedy to a testament to loyalty and what makes a true "Emperor Of The North Pole."

I met Lee Marvin in Bob's office on the Fox lot before filming began on location. There was that squint in his eyes and the so familiar baritone voice as he held court, dissecting his role.

"The guy's a philosopher, a disciple of Kant's metaphysics and ethics, right?"

"Right," I nodded.

"Bull shit."

The man was already in character.

By Now We Know the Line. Which One of Us Says It?

Fearing the audience would misunderstand the title, thinking it was about a trek across the Arctic snow fields, Fox dropped the "Pole," releasing the picture as *Emperor of the North*, to reviews, literally, poles apart. Judith Crist, critic for both *TV Guide* and *New York* Magazine, slammed it, detested it, especially the characters. Vincent Canby of the New York Times saw it differently.

"Christopher Knopf, who wrote the original screenplay, is not without his impulses to set *Emperor Of The North* in larger, more meaningful context (than a king-of-the-hill movie), but usually he resists them. More important, he has created almost perfect action-movie characters, people who can't bore us with their early histories because they don't have any. They exist solely within the time and action of the film itself. When it stops, they vanish, but we have had a sensational ride."

Leonard Maltin followed suit giving it three and a half stars out of four. Regrettably, it didn't achieve much of an audience, though later it sort of did, finding a following mostly among railroad buffs. Some weren't sure they understood the symbolism of it. As Louis B Mayer, late of MGM, once said, "If I could only send the writer around to explain the movie."

Out of it came a dividend, one I wasn't to recognize at first. It started with a call from Bob Eisenbach, my agent. "Be on notice, Fox wants you for a Movie of the Week."

It was to be a television sequel to *Butch Cassidy and The Sundance Kid*. They had no story in mind, just an area for development about what happened to Sundance's girl, Etta Place, following the deaths of the two romantic outlaws in Bolivia. My shoulders sagged. It wasn't something I saw myself doing. I hated the title. *Mrs. Sundance*.

I rarely went to my Father for advice about anything but this time I did. I'm still not sure why. Maybe it was to try and give him a sense of being included. Dad was by now in his mid-seventies, older than his years, could be alternately warm, confused or bellicose, mostly, we'd later discover, due to over-medication for a number of ailments, tranquilizers, sleeping pills, and all those double scotches. At times he was lucid and very much aware which he seemed to be that day as I told him about my assignment offer and my misgivings that it didn't measure up to the sort of thing I saw myself doing.

He sat for a moment, his right hand rubbing the stump of his left wrist.

"It's going to rain."

"Dad?"

"Ethel Barrymore."

"What about her?"

She was one of the incredible gatherings of people that passed through his and my mother's lives.

"Ethel and Louis Calhern were travelling the country doing scenes from Shakespeare."

I hunched forward, wondering what flight of wisdom was going to relate to my query.

"They found themselves performing in a high school gym in Montana one night. They'd been drinking, were into their dialogue, when they suddenly froze. The school librarian who was in the pit whispered the next line. They stared at each other. She whispered it again. They stared at her. In a panic the good woman started to whisper it once more. Calhern raised his hand. 'Madam. By now we know the line. Which one of us says it?'"

I waited for the denouement, the incisive explicative that would make this parable all clear and plain. There was no explicative.

"I don't get it."

"Get what?"

"The point of the story."

Dad frowned, looked at me with genuine bafflement.

"What story?"

Nothing else on my plate, I took the assignment, which turned out to be the beginning of one of the most rewarding relationships of my professional life.

Stan Hough, formerly head of production at Fox, had been brought on as Line Producer of *Emperor Of The North Pole*. A graduate from UCLA, he'd played varsity baseball there, became a professional following graduation, playing in the now defunct Coast League. A six-three, two-hundred thirty-pound iron ingot, they say when he rounded third the infield tilted. Whatever aggression he'd had on the diamond, he left it there. Married to Howard Hughes former wife, the actress Jean Peters, Stan was a total straight arrow, as was Jean, as thoroughly a decent, honorable person I was ever to work with, and work together we did. One feature, two Movies of the Week, and a four-hour mini-series for CBS, with never a tense word between us. At first I barely knew him. Until *Mrs. Sundance*.

It was Stan Hough's idea. He'd gone to Fox following the production of *Emperor of the North Pole* with a concept for a sequel to *Butch And Sundance* as a TV movie, got ABC behind it, and their agreement for me to write it. As in most things there was, as most non professionals who teach writing like to say, an "inciting incident" that solidified our relationship.

My contract signed, I waited for my start payment. Well past due date it hadn't come through. Studios, networks too, often held off paying writers as long as they could, allowing them to draw interest until the last possible moment, even beyond, secure that most writers didn't dare complain. When Stan heard I hadn't been paid, he went down to Fox's business affairs, reached across the desk, grabbed the lead accountant by his shirt front and told him he wanted my check and wanted it now! I got it that day.

Mrs. Sundance was at best a programmer, pure fantasy, Etta Place, hiding away as a small town school teacher, flushed out by bounty hunters, bent on getting her to lead them to the last of Butch and Sundance's gang. You never know where the highs are going to come. Starring Elizabeth Montgomery, it came in second on ABC's Neilson ratings for their television movies that year, all thanks to Elizabeth who was a major television star at the time.

How much of a star? Later, the director Boris Sagal and I went to CBS with an idea for a Movie of the Week. We were turned down. Two weeks later we came back with Elizabeth committed to the project. Deal. Sadly, it never happened as Boris was killed on a pre-production location trip for another show. Deeply preoccupied, he stepped from a helicopter after a surveying flight, and stepped into the rear rotor.

As for Elizabeth, I met her twice, once at the cast reading, again when she appeared in my office door one day during production. She was in costume, and looked incredible.

"You never come down to the set," she said.

I hated going to the set. First, the actors would too often come running, wanting to talk about a line or a scene or their character, which undercut the director's authority. Second, listening to my own lines read was like a golfer, body torquing, willing a wayward shot onto the green. I made up some lame excuse about having pages to get out.

"Too bad," she said, and I swear one eyebrow was raised. "We could have a good time."

To this day I'm still trying to figure out what she meant by that.

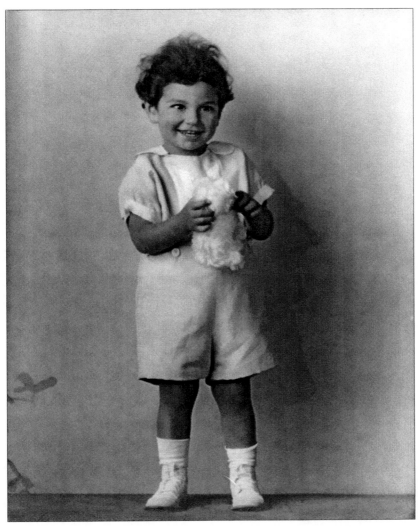

Early Years

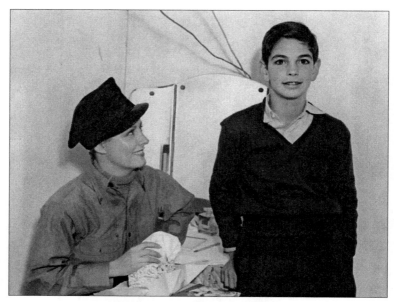

On the set with Irene Dunne

Home on my first leave

Learning the ropes from then Writers Guild President,
Nate Monaster, 1963

President of the Writers Guild, West, 1965

With mother

My brother, Jonathan, Dad and me

Bi-yearly gathering of writers honoring historian, Alan Nevins.
I'm fourth from the right

With co-executive producer, David Simons,
celebrating sale of Equal Justice

My wife, Lorraine, with Timbo

Los Angeles Mayor Tom Bradley with production team of Equal Justice.
L to R, me, Thomas Carter, Bradley, Peter McIntosh, David Simons

With Jane Kaczmarek, co-star of Equal Justice

Notes meeting with Executive Producer, Thomas Carter

Lorraine and I, dressed for Writers Guild Annual Awards dinner

On teaching staff at Sundance. I'm fifth from right

With Hillary Clinton

Friends from the old modeling days at actor, Don Murray's home.
Front, L to R, Millie Perkins, Helen Ryan, Lorraine,
Tippi Hedren. Sandy Comden

L to R, director and former Motion Picture Academy President,
Arthur Hiller, past WGAW President, Del Resiman, Academy Award
winner, Phil Alden Robinson, me, writer and past
Academy President, Fay Kanin, Millard Kaufman

Receiving a WGA Award from writer, Harlan Ellison

The award

The Organization Man

"Be on notice, Kirk Douglas . . . ."

Kirk's company, Bryna Productions, was located behind the Beverly Wilshire Hotel, just up the street from William Morris. I arrived at the appointed time. No Kirk. But there was a large manila envelope waiting for me, Kirk's phone number on it. Read it, I was requested, then call Mr Douglas at home.

The contents revealed a thirty page treatment, titled *Posse*. It was a traditional trek show, a "patrol movie" Robert Aldrich liked to call them, the good guy trying to bring the bad guy in, the bad guys trying to stop him. Mike Dann would have loved it. I didn't. Normally I'd have turned it down, but damn, Kirk Douglas?

We met at his home in Beverly Hills. He couldn't have been more cordial as he ushered me into his unpretentious second floor den. There were no obligatory awards or testimonials or plaques on the walls to dazzle guests that I could see, though he'd earned dozens. From initial meeting to last, I have to admit I was in awe of him. Someone once said there were three men in Hollywood who projected innate, legitimate physical power when in their presence. Burt Lancaster, George C Scott, Kirk Douglas. Not having met the first two, I can vouch for Kirk.

Amenities out of the way, he liked the screen play of *Emperor of the North* as it was now called, which is why I'd been summoned. He asked me what I thought of the treatment. I answered frankly. I thought there wasn't much there, but I had an idea I thought might fit the title.

Several years earlier I'd read a book by Louis Mumford, *The Pentagon Of Power*. In it was a chapter defining the three levels of human condition. At the top would be the "Host Control." The leader, the power source, answerable to no one but himself. At the bottom, the "Drones." The average everyday citizens, who can bleat and whine and moan and shake their fists at the unfairness of it all, but all to little effect. In the middle? The "Organization Man."

Well-trained, obedient, orderly, willing, at the direction of the Host to do his bidding unquestioning, the "Organization Man" was ready to carry out any officially sanctioned fantasy, however dehumanized or debased, as long as never ever being called upon to make a decision about anything, therefore never having to fail. I'd experienced it first hand, once asking a CBS program exec to recommend a writer I thought a lot of to his superiors. He paled, literally, told me flat out, "Don't *ever* put me in a position like that!" There was a story in these people. I just wasn't sure where to place it.

A possible answer came to me one day while working at Universal Studios. I was writing a pilot, given an office across the street outside the studio. I was on my way to the commissary for lunch, which necessitated cutting through the ground floor lobby of the so-called Black Tower, home to Universal's brass. I found myself on a collision course with a suit I'd never met but had seen sitting silently in a group having lunch with Universal's head, Lew Wasserman. He was coming from an elevator, dressed in obligatory black, both of us heading toward the door leading out to the studio lot.

Instinctively I had an antipathy toward suits. Most writers do. You could encounter them on the set, as happened on one of my shows, arriving to tell the director he was running long, to shoot the scene in a single master shot only and get on to the next. The scene in question was an extremely sensitive, revelatory moment in the show that needed coverage. There was no appeal. The suit was there to carry out an order, would not listen, discuss, nor consider anything contrary to it. It was shot as ordered and we lost a truly important moment.

Still, as the suit emerged from the Black Tower elevator that day I had a wave of remorse. Maybe I was being unfairly prejudicial, prejudging this one for the actions of others. He was probably a perfectly lovely fellow, married, with children of his own. What did I really have against him personally? Five seconds later I found out. Reaching the door just ahead of me, he pushed through, let it slam back in my face, affecting at once the disinterest and control of the machine he served. At that moment, so help me God, I had my story. It would be about Universal, the Organization Men of the Black Tower. Kirk's call gave me the venue for it.

In its simplest form, I told Kirk, a highly skilled, trained posse, led by a politically ambitious marshal, captures a wanted outlaw whose gang has been shot out from under him. Escaping capture, the outlaw kills the marshal, is pursued to a town by the posse who finds the outlaw holed up in the town's hotel. With no one to tell them what to do, they try to take up positions, bickering among themselves, unable to coordinate an attack on their own, end up shooting one of the townsmen. It's what the outlaw has planned and been waiting for. Having crossed the line, the posse has no where to go but with the outlaw as his new gang.

Kirk sparked to the idea, saw himself playing the outlaw. As the script progressed, there were meetings, Kirk's instincts good. I always came away energized, but once with a grin on my face.

A call had come in during a meeting from gossip columnist Rona Barrett.

"Kirk," she cooed, her vocal dagger poised to plunge. "Frank gave a party down in Palm Springs last weekend, and you weren't there."

"Geez, I don't know," he replied, "I'm one of the biggies."

It sounded, so help me, like he was doing a parody of himself. Was he putting her on? My guess is yes. Hanging up he went back to the script without a lost beat. It took a lot more than Rona Barrett to shake him.

The script completed, I turned it in, realizing that the third act still needed work. The summons came and we met as usual at his house. True to my intuition it was the third act that bothered Kirk most, but not in the way I'd imagined. He wanted to reverse roles, to play the marshal instead of the outlaw. By doing so, he had no intention of being shot and killed at the end of act two, and out of the rest of the movie. Keep him involved and alive through act three I was told.

I was stunned, and made a colossal mistake. Instead of saying I'd think about that, see what I could do, I defended the concept as written, insisting the purpose of the play was to dramatize the inability of the posse to function without its leader to guide them. Kirk thought a moment, nodded, a nod I didn't properly read.

The next thing I heard about *Posse*, the show was in production, with a rewrite from Bill Roberts. Bill, whom I knew casually, was a fine writer, and when I eventually read his version it was clear he'd pulled off a very good rewrite, the last act especially. I was perfectly willing to share credit with him, he'd earned it, but he wanted sole "Screenplay By" from a story by me. In this he was supported by Kirk, who'd directed the film, Bruce Dern playing the outlaw.

Credits are everything to a screenwriter. Not the least reason, in this case as most, being the bonus I'd get for being included in the "Screenplay By" credit. Bill's claim seemed frivolous. The third act was admittedly his, a genuine contribution, but the entire play? I took him to arbitration through the Writers Guild and won, the two of us sharing "Screenplay By," from a "Story By" me.

As for the picture, it was released at the time of Richard Nixon's downfall, more than one critic citing *Posse* as, in fact, clearly, without contravention, an allegory. About Watergate.

Get Up From That Piano, Boy, You're Hurtin' Its Feelings

"Be in Stan Robertson's office at two thirty." Robertson was program executive of NBC's television movie division.

"Who's this?"

"Stan Hough."

It didn't sound like Stan. The voice was thick and unrecognizable. When I saw him in the NBC lobby I realized why. He looked like he'd taken a high inside fast ball and hadn't ducked. He'd been jogging with his dog that morning. On a leash, it suddenly cut in front of him, going for a squirrel, tripping Stan, who fell to the pavement, knocking out two teeth. Still, he was grinning, which was usual.

Stan Robertson's office was unpretentious, as most network offices are, unlike studios, some of which are palatial. He rose to greet us, a large, grey suited, well kept African-American, the first Black entertainment executive I'd met. Pleasantries concluded, coffee delivered, Robertson webbed his fingers together, looked me over. I had the feeling he had the feeling I wasn't the right writer for this project, whatever it was he had in mind.

"Ever see *The Sting*?" he asked.

I assured him I had, assuming what he had in mind was a television sequel, such as I'd written as a follow up to *Butch and Sundance*.

"What'd you think of the music?"

"Joplin? Loved it."

From what I'd heard, it was George Roy Hill, director of David Ward's clever screenplay, who'd come up with the idea of resurrecting Joplin's turn-of-the-century, mostly forgotten ragtime as background music for the movie.

"We want to do an MOW of his life."

I understood his hesitation. Joplin was Black. I wasn't. Stan jumped in.

"He can do this. He's your guy."

"What do you know about him?" Robertson asked.

"At this point? Nothing," I answered honestly. "What do you have?"

They too had nothing, just his music and name, Berry Gordy's company, Motown, to produce for Universal Studios. Stan Hough went to work. Research was my game, he said. He rattled off what I'd done, especially with *Emperor Of The North Pole*, capturing an unfamiliar world. I could do this, he assured. The look on Robertson's face registered his ambivalence. Were we really the ones to pull this off? Or were we going to put him out of business.

"When can I hear a pitch?" he asked.

I hated that word. Industry slang, it had a cheapness to it. But by agreeing to ask for it the network would have to commit to a full-on no-cut contract, outline, first draft, rewrite and polish. I'd reached a status where I could command it. It was a calamitous investment for them if I turned out a turkey.

"When do you need it?" I asked.

"Yesterday."

It was pre-Google days, so once again it was off to UCLA's North Campus Research Library. Unlike the wealth of material

I'd found earlier on hoboes, there wasn't that much on Joplin, but there was enough. What I found and absorbed gave me, as in *Emperor*, the opportunity to portray a little known world as I saw it. But I needed a theme, something important to me that I could relate to. Without that it was going to be an ordinary biography.

Born in eastern Texas to a family of meager means, Scott Joplin was a piano prodigy. The place for a young Black piano player to find work in the final decades of the nineteenth century were the Black whorehouses up and down the Mississippi.

He wasn't alone. Other young Blacks of the period, virtually all having learned to play by ear, equally found employment in the Black bordellos along the river from New Orleans to St Louis. "Professors," they were called. To the prostitutes they were stars who showered free favors upon them, despairingly leading to syphilis and early deaths for most. It wasn't the only tragedy to befall them. Brilliant as their original compositions were, less than a handful could read or transcribe their music to paper, which sadly died with them.

Joplin was unique, escaping anonymity due to his ability to transcribe his compositions. What he could not escape was syphilis, the "rales," as they called it, which eventually felled him. What happened in between was his meeting John Stark, the white music publisher who took him out of the "tenderloin" and promoted his ragtime, his abandonment of past "professor" friends who offered a decaying image of what his future would be, his marriage and the subsequent death of his only child born to the disease Joplin fought so hard to hide, his rage at not being accepted by white musicologists despite his immense commercial success, his being totally overpowered by John Philip Souza at the 1904 St Louis World's Fair, his break with Stark over his determination to write an opera to gain the approval of white critics.

And there it was. My theme. His battle for approval. All my life it had been a motivating, driving force for me. It wasn't enough that I had to be liked, I had to be venerated for my work. I'd *become* my work. It was the measure of my worth, or lack thereof. And so it was with Joplin as I saw him, even through his deterioration from his worsening disease, Stark coming back into his life near its end, trying to help him raise money for his ill-fated opera that would overcome his lack of recognition as a major American artist.

Completed, the script was turned in to Stan Robertson at NBC. Except Robertson wasn't there any more, fired for reasons unknown to me, again the writer kept in the dark about such things. His replacement was someone I'd never heard of nor was ever to meet, whose first act was to throw out everything Robertson had in development. A serious mistake. He hadn't figured on Motown's Berry Gordy.

Gordy liked the script, and had no interest in appealing his case with Robertson's replacement. Power is as power does, and Gordy had it, and used it, going directly to NBC's head office in New York. The next I heard we were given a go to production and the new west coast program executive was out of the picture, and soon to be out of the network. Billy Dee Williams was signed to play Joplin, Art Carney to play John Stark. Stan produced. Jeremy Kagan directed, and beautifully pulled off one of my favorite moments in anything I'd ever write.

It's the end of the picture. Joplin is playing his operatic score in a rundown theater before a tiny group of potential investors put together by Stark. He starts off well, the music lyrical, beautiful, when suddenly his hands won't perform. Desperately he tries to fight through, but the shattering effect of syphilis destroying his nerves is overpowering. From the wings emerges an old tenderloin friend, Poor Alfred, who gently lifts Joplin's hands from the keys.

"Get up from that piano, boy. You're hurtin' its feelings."

The script was nominated by the Writers Guild for the Best Written Television Movie of the year, awards to be handed out at the annual Writers Guild Dinner at the Beverly Hilton International Ball Room. I invited my parents to be at my table, Dad, taken off his interminable list of numbing medications by a new doctor, back to his old irascible self.

Dinner out with my Father had always proved to be an adventure, usually one that set all of us wanting to dive under the table. Years earlier, invited to the old Beverly Hills favorite, Romanoff's, along with my then wife, Bette, my sister, Wendy, her husband, and my Mother, Dad ordered his usual rare minute steak, French fries and peas.

"Fresh peas," he told the waiter.

"Yes, Mr. Knopf."

"Not frozen."

"Of course, Mr. Knopf."

You knew it was going to happen before dinner arrived. The plate placed before him, Dad leaned forward, sniffed, snapped his fingers for the Maître D.

"Captain!"

"Yes, Mr. Knopf."

"I asked for fresh peas, these are frozen."

By now every table within earshot was glued to the confrontation.

"We wouldn't give you anything but fresh peas, Mr. Knopf."

"Now, I'm mad," Dad said, slapping his right hand on the stump of his left as he sat back in his chair. "Bring me the pods."

The Maître D left, quickly reappeared.

"The pods have been thrown out, Mr. Knopf."

For the rest of the evening he sat in silence, his food untouched as we tried to down ours.

Another time, when I was now married to Lorraine, we took him to the Bel Air hotel for lunch. Rolls arrived, were set on the table.

"Captain!" said Dad, with a snap of his fingers.

"Yes, Mr. Knopf." All the upscale restaurants knew him.

"What do you call these?"

"They're rolls, Mr. Knopf."

At which Dad picked one up, crushed it, bounced it on the floor.

"I call it a tennis ball."

Why this behavior? God knows, and He's kept it His secret. That night, at the Awards Dinner, he was at it again as a dinner of roast beef was served, the waiter setting a plate before him.

"Now I'll tell you what you do," he said imperiously with that slap on his left arm. "You take this back and bring me a nice rare one."

1,700 people to serve, the waiter, who clearly didn't know him from Adam, took his plate, and gave him another of the three he was balancing on his arm, and went on about his business.

Scott Joplin won in its category. When I returned to the table, plaque in hand, there were congratulations from all around. Except Dad. Not a word. He was still stewing over the roast beef, his dinner left untouched.

There was also one other award, more treasured even than the Guild's. I was told by Blacks I knew and met they thought a Black had written the script.

Pure Kismet

"There's got to be someone for me."

"There is."

I was talking to my sister, Wendy. After two failed marriages, the first for eighteen years, the second for three, I was involved in a miserable toxic relationship from which there seemed no exit. My career was going well enough, but not my personal life. Now there was someone for *me?*

"Let me meet her!"

Wendy thought a moment, then uttered a long, slow "Noooo, I don't think so. You haven't suffered enough. You're not ready yet to appreciate a really good woman."

I can do this on my own, I decided. There was a dental hygienist at my dentist's office, and it was time to get my teeth cleaned. She was in her was late twenties, pretty, recently divorced. I lay there, head back, listened to her sad story of her marriage going south, poured on sympathetic charm, as much as able with my mouth wide open. It was clear she was taken with me, and when it was over, when I'd rinsed away the last of my three month collection of tartar, I looked at her. Her eyes were moist with affection.

"I wish," she said, as I waited with expectation, "I had a father like you."

Some have to get a crack on the head to know when enough is enough. Others have to be bloodied. The latter's what happened to me. I was on the phone with the girl friend, in my apartment, in my shorts, in the middle of one of our typical verbal blowouts when I saw blood, literally, flowing down my leg. A hemorrhoid had broken loose.

A call to my proctologist was followed instantly by one to my sister. She relented, released the name. Lorraine Elizabeth Davies. She worked at the Beverly Wilshire, in sales, bringing corporations into the hotel for meetings. She was divorced with three children, ages fifteen to twenty-three, about the same age as mine. Wendy gave me her number.

When Lorraine opened the door, having agreed to meet me at her house one evening, she was, then as now thirty-five married years later, the most beautiful human being I'd ever seen or known. Over prune Danish that night I got her story and she got mine.

Raised in Orlando, Florida, she'd been crowned, at seventeen, Queen of Orlando's Tangerine (now Citrus) New Year's Day Bowl Game in 1945, which earned her a trip to New York where she signed a modeling contract with Conover, a career that lasted twenty years. Divorced, she brought her three children west to California, bought a small house in Santa Monica with the proceeds from the sale of her home in Connecticut. Her income from her days in New York vastly eroded, she went to work as a secretary, then sales rep, head always held high, raising three kids, Rob, Laurie and Andy, on her own, often on dinners at a local hospital cafeteria, because it was the cheapest meal in town. November 11, 1974, a month after we met, I proposed.

"Okay," she said, and it was a thoughtful okay. "But I want a full gestation period first, nine months. I want to know this is going to work."

Two of Lorraine's closest friends were Jim and Lynn Kintzi. Jim was a Lutheran minister, and when Lorraine asked him in late winter of 1974 to perform the marriage ceremony the following June, Jim held back. Lorraine was a Christian, I was not, and Jim was reluctant to marry us unless I'd commit to a life for Christ. Though born to Jewish parents, I'd never had any religious upbringing whatsoever. We'd celebrated Christmas, tree and all. My mother was a closet Catholic, and became one after my father's death in 1981. Still, I felt by acceding to Jim's request I'd be betraying my heritage. I stalled. May came.

"Whatever you decide is alright with me. But you've got to give Jim an answer," Lorraine told me.

I did. I explained I just couldn't do as he asked, and told him why. But I said I'd make a study of it, which I honestly, as I look back on it, had no intention of fulfilling. Jim relented, married us. The fact that I would soon do as I had promised, in a totally unexpected fashion, is pure kismet.

Lorraine, from the time she was eighteen, had always worked. Now able to live on my income, she found herself free to pursue interests she'd never been able to before. She went to college, got a degree, graduating with honors. She got involved in Democratic politics, eventually working for Al Gore, twice met Hillary Clinton, took a screen writing course, wrote two screenplays one of which was optioned. She took lessons in French, sailing and horseback riding, taught aerobics at the local YMCA, went to a women's Bible studies group on the advice of a friend, lasting only a short while as she rejected their antagonism toward gays whom the group considered equal to murderers. One thing came out of it, and she brought it to me. The Biblical story of Peter and Paul. There was great conflict between the two, a film there, she thought.

I'd had about as much to do with the Bible as I had with Das Kapital; I'd never studied either. I hummed a "Gee, nice," and went about other matters, till a phone call from Stan Hough. Procter and Gamble, through CBS, wanted to do a four-hour mini-series to be filmed in Greece. They'd come to Stan to produce it. Stan recommended me to write it. They said okay. The topic? Peter and Paul.

Lorraine of course was thrilled, convinced it must have been due to some extrasensory powers of transmutation. I was stunned and baffled. How was I to write such a thing with Christians, even Jews, world wide, peering over my shoulder? I had no great passion for religion. And what was in it for me? I don't mean financially, I mean thematically, which, as discussed, has always been important in anything I've tried to write, my reason for doing so, for wanting to do so. What exploration was there for me that could lead me into and through a 240-page script of one of the greatest events ever written? What mystery was there for me to uncover, if only for myself, upon which to build a drama?

I read the New Testament cover to cover. Peter's story was pretty straightforward. Not so Paul's. Born a Roman citizen in Tarsus outside the borders of Palestine, Saul (his Hebrew given name) rose through his youth to become a brilliant Talmudic scholar, was sent to Jerusalem to study further with the eminent Rabban, Gamaliel.

There, however, he found himself assigned to the bloody mission of ferreting out the nascent sect of so-called Christians, a Roman term of contempt meaning "Christ followers". In fact Saul first appears in Biblical record as a witness to the stoning of Stephen, the first martyr to the cause of Christ, even "consenting" to Stephen's death. The fear of Saul among these early Christians was significant; though it's assumed he thought he was doing Jehovah's will.

Armed with arrest warrants, he departed with a convoy for Damascus to continue his purging. En route the Bible describes the immensely powerful moment when there's a burst of light, so terrifying it throws Saul from his mount, and he hears Christ's voice demand, "Saul, Saul, why do you persecute me?" Blinded, Saul's taken to Damascus, fasts, unseeing for three days. And therein begins his conversion, and the change to his Christian name, Paul.

Half the world accepts Christ's condemnation of Saul on that road as the unimpeachable basis for his turning to Christianity, but the Bible states clearly that none of Saul's companions heard Christ's voice that day. Only Saul, and only Luke in "Acts" records it, who would have had to hear of it from the one and only source, Paul.

Many people, alcoholics, condemned men, prisoners, failures, the dying, the hopeless, have hit the bottom of despair so deep they've turned to Christ with no place else to turn. My late brother was one. Having conned and wasted his way through life, known bankruptcy, jail, virtually cut off from his father from whom he stole and hocked the family silverware, his life in a downward spiral, suddenly sought and found salvation in Jesus Christ. Saul, highly trained to do God's work, his life committed to it, found all he'd worked for, trained for, wrested from him, to be abandoned, ordered into savagery and destruction by the Sanhedrin. Disciplined, he did the Sanhedrin's bidding, all that it asked. On the road to Damascus to continue this work, he suddenly had a personal violent upheaval, rebelling against all he'd now become, which is what I believe happened. That Christ spoke to him, it's certainly probable he believed it.

There was no way, however, Procter and Gamble, CBS, nor the public would accept anything from me other than the literal Biblical interpretation which I'd have to write without personal conviction.

I consulted Lorraine, told her of my quandary, my belief that Paul's conversion, like all conversions, was brought about from despair, not Holy intervention.

"Read Acts," she said.

"I've read it."

"Read it again."

And there it was, the contradiction to my thinking. Luke.

Born in Macedonia, Luke was a physician, whose curative powers, by training, amounted to cotton, honey and the laying on of hands. Seemingly educated, perhaps an intellectual, he was enough so to eventually write one of the most remarkable accounts in world literature, Biblical or otherwise.

Luke was also a Greek, by upbringing an idolater, a worshiper of graven images. Upon meeting and joining Paul in his travels to Rome, Luke abandoned his heritage, turned to Christianity, his conversion brought about by no personal trauma, but solely by observation of events. Contrary to my rigid conclusions, that was fascinating, an unfolding mystery for me to explore. I would take the journey with Luke, witness what changed him and why, which is what I did. It didn't convert me as it did Luke, but it opened my mind to a concept of conversion I had not been willing to consider.

Finished, the script was turned into Procter and Gamble and CBS. Both accepted it without a call for significant rewrites, but there were two flies in the ointment.

First, before it could be approved for production, every major religion in the country had to be satisfied with it as written. Some conservative evangelists wouldn't even read it, claiming we had no authority to interpret the word of God. The Catholics and Protestants got into it over James, the brother of Jesus, who the Bible clearly states, and as I dramatized, kept the Christian embers alive in Jerusalem after Christ's death till the emergence of Paul. The Catholics objected to calling James Christ's brother, insisting Mary was virginal throughout her life, therefore had no other children.

"What was James then if not a brother?"

"A cousin," I was told.

"Like John the Baptist?"

"Yes."

"Then why does the Bible refer to James as a brother and John the Baptist as a cousin? Why not both the same?"

The Jews felt anti-Semitism came solely from the New Testament, that without it, it wouldn't have occurred, and wanted to be sure we'd do nothing to fan the flames. Feathers were smoothed, assurances given, and all ended serenely.

Not so our second fly. An Italian producer, a Produttore, had been hired by Proctor and Gamble as a consultant on the development of Peter and Paul. We met at Stan Hough's house, Stan, I, the Produttore, and a representative from P and G. The Produttore opened the meeting.

The script, he intoned, was unusable, required a major rewrite, we'd never be able to cast it. Solution? Bring in another writer of Produttore's choosing.

It was the first time I'd laid eyes on him. Whatever service he was to have provided us during the script's development never happened. Never heard from him, never saw him, nor met him till then.

It was clear what he was doing, trying to get out from under his lack of performance in front of Proctor and Gamble, and Stan and I knew it. With Proctor and Gamble looking back and forth between Stan and him as though at a tennis match, trying to discern whom to believe, Stan verbally drove the Produttore into the wall. CBS liked the script. Proctor and Gamble liked the script. He accused him of trying to create a false crisis to deflect his noncompliance.

When the meeting was over the Italian was out of our hair. At least, out of mine. Bringing Bob Day aboard to direct, we entered a phase we'd been told we couldn't, casting. Eddie Albert was signed to play Festus, the Roman general who sent Paul to Rome. Raymond Burr as Herod Agrippa. Jose Ferrer as Gamaliel. John Finch, Herbert Lom, Jean Peters, John Rys-Davies. Robert Foxworth would play Peter. For Paul? Anthony Hopkins.

Contrary to our Italian's expectations, the public's reaction was astonishingly positive. "A great movie." "Never seen Anthony Hopkins better." "One of the best biblical movies." "Highly recommended." "Literate script." "Wonderful moments."

As for Biblical dramas, how do you guarantee their success? First start with an English actor.

Scraping the Bottom of the Barrel

Four times in my fifty years writing for motion pictures and television I went to arbitration over credits. Usually the process is straight forward, as it was with *Posse*. Everyone, who feels they've been denied a proper credit as suggested by the production company, has the right to submit their material to three arbiters, all professional writer members of the Guild, the Guild alone having authority to determine credits. Unknown to each other, the arbiters independently come to a determination after reading, in order, all scripts written for the project, measuring it against the final screenplay. Two out of three rules. But sometimes the process can become incredibly messy, as were two of mine.

CBS had run a piece on *Sixty Minutes* on the infamous George Parr, a member of the political family which controlled a Democratic Party machine that dominated Duval County in southeast Texas. Parr engaged not only in graft, bribery and fraud, but was rumored to have had political enemies murdered. His most infamous act of political corruption was browbeating election officials in nearby Jim Wells County into providing invalid votes of even dead people to ensure the primary victory of Lyndon Johnson in the U.S. senatorial election of 1948. Relying on a sizeable fortune, his handpicked candidates continued to sweep county elections until his death by suicide in 1975, thereby bringing collapse to the Parr machine.

A television movie based on the *Sixty Minutes* profile was put into development, Robert Greenwald and Frank Von Zerneck to produce, Howard Koch to executive produce, three highly respected and accomplished talents. I was asked to write the script. I despised manipulation of human beings for personal gratification and power, looked forward to portraying it through the life and chicanery of a genuinely despicable man.

Not so fast.

Following the dictates of CBS's legal department, we couldn't use Parr's name, or the name of his county. We couldn't mention Lyndon Johnson. We could dramatize Parr's tactics, control and graft, but with a made up name in a made up county. The story would have to be totally fictitious. So much for George Parr who *was* the story, the reason for doing it.

There are some projects I simply should not have taken. On this one I should have trusted my stomach, and it was churning. Further, I couldn't find my way into the piece as reconstructed. Going after a real life villain was one thing. A made up one put it in the category of usual and ordinary.

All those attached, however, were highly regarded, so the word "pass" stuck in my throat. Maybe I was guilty of arrogance that I could make anything work. I tried. George Parr became Ambler Bowman. Duvall County became Bogen County. The script became a fictitious account of Bowman's much younger wife trying to escape the dominance and control of her husband aided by a single Texas Ranger who takes on Bowman on her behalf. Thus the title, *Escape From Bogen County*. The script wasn't great, maybe not very good, but it worked well enough to pass judgment by the producers and be sent on to CBS for approval. We were called to a meeting.

As I had encountered with *Scott Joplin*, the executive who'd ordered the project had been replaced. In his chair was now Paul Monash. I'd known Paul for years. Giving him his due, he'd written some of the best television on record, was a multiple awards nominee and winner. As an executive he was wanting, difficult, mercurial and dictatorial. That Paul did not last long in the job is history. But he had it that day, and we were answerable to him.

He wanted a rape in the script, and it wasn't open to debate.

I stared at him. Why? I don't recall that he gave a reasonable answer, at least none that I can remember. He wanted a rape. All eyes were on me. Producers in the television world, those days at least, seldom received a dime until a script was ordered for production, unlike the writer who was and is paid whether or not his script is usable. If I said no to Paul these producers would probably receive nothing unless they could move the script forward with somebody else. But I hated the idea, it had no place in the show, lent nothing to the dramatic impact that wasn't already there. Further the character of Bowman I'd written would never reduce himself to rape, it was beneath him. His magnetism and power and the fear he projected was such, in his mind, he would never have to. What I hated most was Paul's reason for demanding it. He was establishing his authority. I gave my reasons for opposing it, told Paul, no, I couldn't do that. Sorry, but no.

The picture was rewritten by a young woman writer I knew of but had not met. Once filmed, the production company suggested she and I share credit. I read her script, saw a lot of dialogue changes, and there was the rape, but otherwise no change in characterizations, story or structure. I told the Guild I'd go with the company's suggested determination, shared credit, assumed the second writer would agree. She didn't. She wanted sole credit, the Guild told me, and was going to arbitration for it. I asked the Guild if I was allowed to speak to her. The Guild gave me her number.

On the phone she was adamant. The script was hers. I was leaving for Europe with Lorraine the following morning, and I didn't want to have to spend the night writing my statement supporting my position for an arbitration panel if it could be avoided. I'd share credit with her, which is the most she would get. She held firm. It was her script, she insisted, she'd written it, she deserved all the credit. If she forced me into that letter, I told her, to give up my night when I should be packing, I was going for full credit myself, and I'd win it, citing her limited changes. She hung up, clinging to her position.

I won the arbitration, was awarded sole credit by the committee. The whole thing. Written by me. She was devastated. I called the Guild and told them, give her half credit. The Guild had never heard of such a magnanimous thing, asked why? Magnanimous? Not close. Because, I answered, when the reviews came out they were going to be so awful I wanted her to suffer the same as I. Writing in *TV Guide*, Judith Crist opened her review of *Escape From Bogen County*, with "Scraping the bottom of the barrel this week . . . ."

All of which was nothing compared to *Choir Boys*. I'd gotten a call from Robert Aldrich who'd directed *Emperor Of The North Pole*. Had I read the Joe Wambaugh book? I had. Wambaugh, an ex-detective turned author, had written several successful books drawn from his experiences with the Los Angeles Police Force. *Choir Boys* followed a group of cops, assigned to narcotics, trying to shed some of the ugliness and pressure of their jobs by engaging in various forms of after-hours debauchery. It was a good, insightful novel.

Bob had a script by Wambaugh, he told me, adapted from his book, that needed a new ending. He asked to meet.

The meeting took place at Merv Adelson's Bel Air canyon home. Adelson, Lee Rich, Aldrich and I. The first thing I noticed was the house. It was set against a high-rising cliff, far back from the road with a gated entry. It was not a place of easy access. It was built for security.

I knew Lee, had met him several years earlier, summoned to Hollywood's famed Chasen's Restaurant for dinner one night to discuss projects. A former New York advertising executive, just arrived in Los Angeles. to make his mark in the industry, he did not come without the tools of his trade as Chasen's well known little person, Johnny, dressed in his famed Philip Morris costume, circled the room calling out for all the moguls and power brokers present to hear.

"Telephone call for Mr Lee Rich! Telephone call for Mr Lee Rich!"

The call, I quickly learned, came from his secretary telling Lee there were no messages. Despite liking him, awed by his chutzpah and energy, I remember thinking, "You better have more than that going for you." Lee did, forming, along with Merv Adelson, one of the most successful television companies ever created, Lorimar Telepictures, Lee serving as executive producer on a host of mega hits, *The Waltons, Eight Is Enough, Dallas,* and *Knots Landing.*

As for Adelson, we'd never met, but I knew him by reputation. Everyone did. Or thought they did. It was fact vs rumor, and no one seemed to really know the truth. It all supposedly began in Vegas, Adelson's first business a grocery store. Next he was building houses around a casino, which grew into more real estate ventures. His most famous? La Costa, the famed California resort for the super affluent. It was there that rumors began he was in or associated with the mob. If not, he certainly rubbed shoulders with colorful characters.

But the big goal for Adelson was Hollywood. A thrill seeker who loved helicopter-skiing in the mountains, he clawed his way to the top of the Hollywood heap, meeting mobsters and movies stars, presidents and royalty, married beautiful women, emerging as a Hollywood heavy hitter by joining forces with Lee Rich in forming Lorimar. For all this I found a genuine lack of artifice in the man, at least around me. I liked him.

The assignment I was being asked to perform was laid out quickly. The end of Wambaugh's screenplay, a literal adaptation of his novel, was simply too despairing, too negative, I was told. It needed, if not an upbeat, at least a hopeful finish. I was being asked to provide one.

There is a phenomenon in this business, and for the first and only time in my career I profited from it. Once a screenplay is "green lit" as they say, ordered for production, money flows. I was offered and paid more for rewriting the final three pages of *Choir Boys*, which is all I wrote and was asked to write, than I was for the entire original screen play of *Posse*.

The rewrite completed, the show was shot and Wambaugh went ballistic. Not only did he hate the ending, which he announced completely ruined his intent, but there was a clause in his contract prohibiting anyone other than him from doing any writing or rewriting on *Choir Boys* without his consent, which had neither been asked for nor granted.

I had not been told that. Had I been I never would have accepted the assignment, but Wambaugh was on a tear. He ranted about suing Lorimar, blasted me, claimed I'd butchered his creation, reportedly sent a communiqué to a major executive at Universal, co-producers with Lorimar of the movie, condemning me personally. One thing he made eminently clear. He wanted his name off the picture.

If only that had been the end of it. Anything to unload my association with the project, and with Wambaugh. It wasn't to be. A conference call from Lee Rich and Merv Adelson came in. 98 percent of the script being Wambaugh's, they wanted me to fight him through the Guild on this, to take him to arbitration, not to ask for credit for myself, but to insist that Wambaugh be made to take it himself. Their reason? His name on the show was essential as a major marketing tool.

Never in the history of the Guild had there been such an arbitration: two writers fighting, not to *claim* credit for themselves, but to force the *other* to take it. Wambaugh won. His claim he had the right to remove his name from the project, from any project, was upheld by Guild rules. At the same time he was severely admonished not to continue his personal attack on another member of his Guild as he had been doing.

When Lee Rich and Merv Adelson heard the verdict, they called me again, insisted I go back to the Guild and demand a review of the decision. It was an emotional call. I'd hit the wall over this and wanted no further part in it. Adelson persisted. Lee, sensing he'd pushed me as far as he should, gratefully called it quits.

The picture was finished and released to less than complimentary notices. For all Wambaugh's public statements ridding himself of any and all responsibility, one major critic called him on it, citing him as being far more responsible for it's content than he was willing to admit.

As for me? I let my name go on the film as the sole writer of the screenplay, which was ridiculous. For three pages? Some name had to go there. As a reward or not, Lee hired me to develop and write a series pilot for Lorimar, which was shot with Brian Dennehy in the lead. When it made it to a network schedule Lee called me into his office.

"Are you interested in going under contract to Lorimar?"

I told him that sounded interesting.

"Are you prepared to do that now?"

I told him I was. He asked the name of my agent. I told him that too.

"You'll be hearing from me," he said.

I never heard from Lee Rich again.

I'm Terribly Sorry, Sir, But Are We Acquainted?

December 27, 1981. It was a Sunday. Dad and I were sitting in his tiny den on Mandeville Canyon, watching a professional football game. It had become a ritual, Sunday's game on television, all the more important now as the teams vied for the post season playoffs. It almost hadn't come to pass.

"If he has the surgery, he could die on the table. If he doesn't have it, he will."

That had been two years earlier. We were in the doctor's office, Mother, my sister, Wendy, my brother, Jonathan, Lorraine and I. Dad, seventy-nine, had been diagnosed with an embolism and a severely infected gall bladder. If there was to be surgery, both would be done at the same time. He could die on the table. If the surgeries weren't performed? He would die. It was a family decision and it was made. Surgery.

A series of mini strokes had altered Dad's disposition and personality. For the most part he'd become docile and vague, and with it a certain unaccustomed sweetness had come over him. It was as though, with the strokes, all the furies that had beset him all his life had been eased or erased. Yet there were complications. On more than one occasion he'd addressed me, sitting with him in his den with, "I'm terribly sorry, sir, but are we acquainted?" Sometimes he would get up from his chair and announce, "I want to go home, now." The thing to do was put him into a car, drive him around the neighborhood, ask him where he lived, and follow his directions back to his house.

Or the times he'd come from his bedroom, a stack of his treasured silk handkerchiefs under arm and head for the car.

"Dad, where you going?"

"I'm going to New York."

Or when he'd get loose, out of the house, and disappear, to be discovered seated, a half mile away, elegantly dressed in coat and tie, propped up in a chair at some curb where a kindly neighbor had placed him to be found.

Or the day Mother called on a rainy Saturday morning, telling me he'd gotten out the back door to the garden, had fallen from the steps, was lying between the house and the camellia bushes. Rushing over, I found Mother, still in nightgown, hovering over him with an umbrella, Dad lying there with two broken ribs.

"Dad, how you doing?" I asked as I tried to figure out how to get him up.

"I'm in the pink," he answered almost jovially.

Pain was one thing he'd always tolerated with incredible courage. If his box of Kleenex wasn't where it was supposed to be, on the table next to his chair in the den, he'd bring the house down. But pain? Never a frown or a groan. Such as now as he lay in his hospital bed the night before his double surgery.

The entire family was gathered. He seemed at ease. Every doctor he'd ever gone to was, in his words and mind, a "giant of medicine." He wouldn't, of course, consider anything less, so he was at peace. Until the anesthesiologist arrived.

Telling Dad, as he was bound to by law, all the surgery entailed, including the horribles that could be encountered during and after the surgery, Dad listened with an increasingly appalled look on his face. When the anesthesiologist was gone, Dad reached for his cane, unsteadily swung his feet down, rose, butt flap open, headed out of his room and down the hall.

"Dad?"

"I'm going home!"

The surgery went remarkably well, Dad, to the amazement of all, his doctors included, surviving. And now we were sitting there watching the game. He frowned in confusion.

"Do you understand what they're doing?" he asked me.

I explained as best I could.

"I just don't understand what they're doing."

Our relationship had mellowed. He never made any reference to the business in which he'd spent so many years of his life, nor asked questions about what I had done or was doing, nor made reference to it. He loved Lorraine. Any time she came around he'd perk up. But conversation could be bizarre. He'd start a sentence, and lose the thought half way through, which never seemed to bother him. The game over I got up. He'd taken to kissing my cheek when I left, which he did then. At seven thirty that night I received a call from Mother. He was watching Lena Horne on *Sixty Minutes*, a broad grin on his face. Mother turned away for a moment, turned back to find him slumped in his chair. He was gone.

When Dad had lost his position at Metro he'd lost eighty percent of his friends overnight. It was as though his demise was contagious. And now, twenty-two years later, they all turned up at his funeral. It was an industry "do" and no one wanted their name omitted from the coverage of it in *Variety* and the *Reporter*. My Mother was livid.

As for myself, there was a certain melancholy to it all. It was as though the main issue between us, my success and his lack of acknowledgment of it, had never been addressed. Until one day.

He'd been gone several weeks, his ashes scattered at sea. I'd been going through his papers at Mothers' request, deciding what should be kept, what should be trashed. It was there I found a Xeroxed copy of some correspondence he'd written on his personalized stationary to a critic.

"Dear Sir," it began. "I have just read your review of *Loudmouth*, the outstanding television program (your words) presented last night. You praise the star, Jack Lemmon. You praise the director, Donald McDougal, and supporting actor, Harold Stone. Nowhere in your review do you mention the superb effort of the writer, Christopher Knopf, my son. I can only assume you ran out of ink."

The critic responded with a dismissive note. It was clear, he wrote back, words, if not whole speeches, in the play were adlibbed. To which Dad returned the critic's note, affixing to the bottom of it, "Some idiot wrote this over your signature." It was signed, Edwin H. Knopf.

Shaking Hands With the Pope

There's an old, weathered hotel, "Sylvia's," beaten grey by wind-driven sand on the beach in Newport, Oregon. Two features are unique about the place. First, every guest room is dedicated to an American author, each with a separate mini-library of the writer's books. Hemingway, Willa Cather, Steinbeck, Faulkner. Second, in the basement dining room, at dinner, seated at long tables of six or eight over fresh caught salmon, you're asked to play a game. Tell three stories about yourself. Two are true, one is a lie. Questions are then asked. You must answer the truthful ones truthfully, and make the lie sound true. People then vote. Which is the lie?

My three, when it came to me were: I was a speech writer for Lyndon Johnson; I had a date with Elizabeth Taylor; I shook hands with the Pope.

True enough, I did have a date with Elizabeth Taylor, when she was seventeen and I was twenty, though "date" is a bit of a stretch. I escorted her with my parents to dinner and a play, my father producing *Cynthia*, a movie starring Elizabeth at the time. I remember walking her down the aisle toward our seats. Every eye in the place was on us. She was very much a teenager then, and despite her fame and beauty, pleasant, respectful, demure, and, showing good judgment, not the least interested in me.

Of the two that were left, I was *not* a speech writer for President Johnson, though I was for Alan Cranston, along with two other writers, Nate Monaster and David Karp, when Cranston first ran for the Senate in California. The three of us, all active in Democratic politics, were summoned to pen Cranston's speech on Viet Nam. It was 1968, the war full on. Cranston was totally opposed to it, but tentative about saying so. Seated with his inner circle of advisors, we listened to them tell us what they wanted in the speech as Cranston stood across the room at the bar, filling his glass. Finally I broke their narrative and asked:

"What's the candidate think?"

"We'll *tell* him what he thinks," they answered. Welcome to Poli Sci One.

The one true story left, I did shake hands with the Pope, an event that was bizarre in itself. But that's what I did. What led to it? It began in Bernie Sofronski's office, four years earlier, 1981, at CBS.

Sofronski, who would one day compile a portfolio as executive producer of superior television movies and mini-series, was then head of CBS Specials. A call from my agent, "Be on notice . . . ." had led to a meeting with Alvin Cooperman and his partner Judith de Paul, New York-based producers who, in partnership with CBS, had a deal to develop a three hour dramatic special on the life of then Pope John Paul II. I was being asked to write it.

They had to be kidding. *Peter and Paul* had been daunting enough, but now I was to put words in the mouth of a living revered Holy Father? Alvin and Judith had come west to meet with me and the network. Their television producing credits were elegant and eclectic. *But John Paul II?*

Lean, serious, vaguely intellectual, Sofronski had two associates with him at the meeting. One, if memory serves, had been involved mostly with network revues and comedy specials. The other, a young development executive named Greg Mayday, would one day become the salvation of the project.

In the meeting I was respectful but blunt. I knew nothing about the Pope, and told them so, other than the fact he was Polish, and that he'd somehow broken the choke hold of the Italians on the Papacy. My strong suit was research and there was a Monsignor at St Monica's Catholic Church in Santa Monica I'd met who'd studied in Rome. I thought he might be willing to spend some time with me, but I just didn't know.

They pushed hard. Think of the drama of it all, the contrast, theater student, athlete, the girls and women in his life before the priesthood. And then the war, joining partisans in the woods with their raids against the Germans. Great story, all there. I finally said I'd be willing to accept the assignment with a proviso. Either one of us, the network or I, could terminate my employment at story, which was contrary to the usual no cut contracts I always had. My purpose? After writing a treatment I wanted an out, even if the network wanted me to continue, if I felt, for whatever reason, I'd be embarrassing myself, or them, by continuing. It was a no-lose proposition for CBS. They took it.

Over lunch with Alvin and Judith following our meeting, I fell for these two. Their language was theater, which was their background. Where this would lead us I just didn't know. But I loved where they wanted to go.

"Don't be intimidated," they entreated me. "Don't hold back. But don't manufacture what isn't there. Most of all, don't double think the network. Get into the research and develop the story as dramatically, but factually as you can."

When I was ready, they added, there was a priest, Father Jadoff, in Manhattan, who had responsibility from the Vatican to approve the script, and another on Staten Island considered the leading authority on the Pope in the country. They'd fly me to New York for meetings with both.

My never-fail fount of information had always been the north campus research library at U.C.L.A., and it didn't fail me now. There were books on Karol Wojtyla, (his name pre John Paul II), on his life as a youth in Poland and Poland itself before, during and after the war. There were books on the German occupation, then Russian. Others on his becoming a priest, his reluctant rise in the church, and Catholicism in Poland, and its history. Still others on the politics of the Vatican and the Curia, and most important of all, the scandal that led to Wojtya being voted, by default, Pope over two favored Italian Cardinals, Siri and Bonelli, who'd gone after each other in public just before the convocation and thereby eliminated themselves.

The most pressing question to answer was what turned this vigorous, brilliant scholar-athlete with a burning ambition of becoming an actor to the priesthood? There was also the usual question, what was in it for me?

It took three weeks, but I thought I'd found the answer to both, which, if right, would give me the driving conflicted force Wojtya faced from boyhood to the day of his coronation, and my reason for wanting to explore his story. *How could anyone, beginning with his youth, born into modest circumstances, through war and occupation and opposition, know who he was and never, till the day of his coronation, deviate from that?*

Arriving in New York with Lorraine, I left her to visit friends while I went first to meet Father Jadoff. He was not what I expected. Young, athletic, matinee idol good looks, he said, "Come on. Let's take a walk."

Along the streets of Manhattan I told him what I thought I'd discovered about Karol Wojtyla, his reasons for joining the priesthood. Catholicism, going back centuries, had always been the driving force in Poland. So much so that newly crowned kings were made to crawl on their hands and knees in obeisance to the Holy Virgin. Priests, and the hierarchy of the Church, had a most prominent position of influence in Polish culture. I told Father Jadoff I believed that Wojtyla, who turned to the priesthood rather later than most, did so during the latter part of the German occupation, recognizing that following the war there would be a battle for the souls and minds of Polish youth, especially with the Communists if the Russians took over, which they did. The war over, with the Russians now occupying Poland, young Father Wojtyla would take students, male and female, into the mountains on camping trips, where they were free to discuss their confusions about what and whom to believe, away from the prying eyes and ears of teachers, parents and authorities. Further, when offered the promotion to bishop, he'd tried to refuse it, not wanting to give up his work with the young. In short I thought Wojtyla, who deeply loved his country, became a priest to preserve it.

Father Jadoff thought a moment, nodded, said he thought I might be on to something, told me to go with it as we passed two pretty young women who looked him over.

"How do you handle that?" I asked.

"That," he answered with a smile and shake of his head, "can be a problem."

That afternoon, Alvin Cooperman, Lorraine and I met, as

planned, with the Staten Island priest considered America's leading authority on John Paul II. I say "considered," because as we sat
in his dank dining hall having a spare lunch of finger sandwiches,
it quickly became clear I knew more about the Pope's youth and
years in Poland than he did. His knowledge of the man was Rome.
Karol Wojtya's story, as I conceived it, *ended* in Rome.

The treatment accepted by CBS, with admonitions not to for-
get the girls and the Germans, I took a deep breath and dug into
a 180-page, three-hour teleplay. Greg Mayday was the one who
stayed the course with me throughout the script.

Met that first day in Sofronski's office, Greg was an anomaly
among most network executives, one of whom, years earlier, had
capped a meeting with, "Let's run it up the flagpole and see if the
cat laps it up." Scholarly, steeped in literature and drama, deeply
concerned with digging into a subject to achieve the best possible
result, Greg was one I could call and say, "I'm stuck!"

If I were to give advice to neophyte writers I'd say that is the
one thing never, ever do, tell a network executive mid-stream
you're stuck. You'll see exploding lights, hear sirens, possibly see a
body hurling itself from a top floor window, certainly your agent
will get a panicked call. Not Greg.

"Come on up," he'd say. "Let's get it."

The script completed it was turned into the network and a
meeting was called by Sofronski. Usually when there's excitement,
when things are going well, you'll be given a parking place next to
the building. This day I was assigned a half day's walk to the entrance. There was going to be trouble.

Entering Sofronski's office I quickly learned what. His associ-
ate did the talking. Where were the girls? There were no girls! And

his activities with Polish partisans, hunting down, killing Nazis! Where was that?

I took them one at a time. In all my research I'd found no significant relationships with any girls as a youth, nor women as a young man. The closest was when he was working, during the war, in a rock quarry. There apparently was a young woman, Hanna, in the office who took to him, which was explored in the script. He considered her a friend but there was nothing more he offered the relationship that either I nor anyone else could uncover.

As for his joining partisans, going after Germans, it never happened. As a matter of fact he was in conflict with the partisans' activities, feeling all energies should be guided toward the future when the war would end. There was an aggressive scene I'd written of confrontation between Wojtyla and a young partisan leader, Powel, dramatizing their separate philosophies. That Wojtyla had pacifist tendencies is possible. What he *did* do, however, was join an underground network actively involved in getting Jewish families out of their homes to safety when word was received through the underground of upcoming German block raids, which was dramatized in the script.

"We'll call you," I was told by Sofronski, which of course, is a eulogy for most projects. Except it wasn't, all credit due to Greg Mayday.

With Sofronski retiring shortly thereafter from CBS Specials, moving on to his own successful projects, the division was taken over by Marian Brayton. Marian, who would later become executive of a run of her own distinguished television films, not only inherited CBS Specials, she inherited Greg Mayday with it. All credit to Greg, he kept the dying ember of *John Paul II* alive, stoked it till it became a flame with Marian and was finally ordered into production. It was the first of four CBS Specials I did with Marian, who proved to be the best, most supportive network executive I ever worked with along with Stan Kallis.

Of all the shows ever produced from a script of mine, *John Paul II* turned out to be, for me, the most beautifully realized. Directed by Herb Wise, who'd directed *I, Claudius*, it starred Albert Finney as Wojtyla, Alvin and Judith mounting a remarkable production, which was almost shut down mid-stream.

While filming in Rome, the Yugoslavian government, which had given permission for the company to shoot the Polish sequences inside its country, decided, literally a week beforehand, to pull the plug. Its antipathy toward the Vatican, and the church's conflict with the Communists as dramatized in my script, were after all beyond tolerance. No filming in Yugoslavia. Scrambling, and scrambling fast, the Polish sequences were transferred to Austria. Thankfully locations turned out to be gorgeous.

Reviews were positive, Leonard Maltin acknowledging "Finney's American television acting debut allows him to add another memorable portrait to his diverse gallery of colorful full-bodied portrayals. A reverential tour-de-force."

Another reviewer caught what had drawn me to Carol Wojtyla's story, citing it as the portrayal of "a man who confronts his feelings under the guidance of wisdom, reason and faith, who accepts responsibilities with humility and trust." The script was nominated by the Writers Guild.

As for shaking hands with the Pope, it happened on his trip to the United States. He'd come to Los Angeles to address the leaders of Hollywood, which took place at Universal Studios. I was invited, seated in the audience, a hundred feet away. Speaking in English, one of nine languages he knew, John Paul II concluded his remarks by walking down the roped off center aisle. People pressed to the rope, offering their hands, which he took as he made his way out. I couldn't get to the rope, but thrust my hand through between people, and—he took it! Never saw me, I never saw him, but he took it! I didn't wash that hand for a week.

What Magic Are You Going to Weave for Me?

"Judy, while you're resting, get us some coffee."

I was in Jerry Leider's office, president of ITC Entertainment, an independent television company in the Valley. I was being asked if I'd be interested in going under contract, but the coffee request, for the moment, held me. It was made by Leider's second in command to a third executive in the room. She was the least in rank of the three. But she was a person of purpose, and, as an executive, junior or otherwise, not someone to send for coffee. Near forty, chic and trim in tailored business suit, notebook in hand, her face tightened with what seemed embarrassment and resentment. She nodded, rose and left the room to comply. Her name I'd learn was Judith Polone, her responsibility, so far as I understood, was new projects. I would eventually realize she was bright and driven, but at that moment only one thought went through my mind. *No good was going to come of this.*

I was given an office and an assignment, a rewrite of a three-hour special for CBS. It was the true story of a woman in Kansas City, Katherine Bauer, who ran a clinic for third world children with severe heart conditions, bringing them from their countries to America for surgery, returning them to their homes when well.

Taking place during the Viet Nam war, a group of sick children were to arrive from Saigon still thought to be safely in U.S. hands. When the children didn't arrive as scheduled Katherine Bauer travelled there herself to bring them out, found conditions deteriorating far more than advertised, American civilians fleeing the country, grabbing all available transportation out for themselves. Meeting a Vietnamese, exiled from his country who had sneaked back in to find his own three children, the two joined forces, both failing to get their respective children on a flight as the Viet Cong attacked the city, the two herded against their wills aboard the last transport plane out.

The story was a saga of two people's developing love for each other, bound as they were by mutual loss, their ultimate marriage, and never ending efforts to find at least his children and bring them safely to America, which they eventually did under incredible circumstances.

It was a great story, though I had concerns that the American public would not tolerate such a relationship. Judy assured me the network was totally behind the project, especially as Lee Remick was attached to it. I was to learn networks are always at their most courageous in development, less so at the time of decision.

The script they had, Judy knew, and I discovered upon reading it, regrettably was soft, too often cliché, the characters unrealized, as was the drama. A luncheon meeting was set up with Lee Remick at the Hotel Bel Air to discuss changes.

Meetings, especially first meetings with stars over projects, potential or in existence, are a mixed bag. Unable to speak for others, I can only offer my own experience. Robert Mitchum was arrogant and contemptuous. Stuart Whitman suspicious. Lee Marvin oblique and indecipherable. Kirk Douglas brilliant but controlling. Barbara Stanwyk, compassionate but firm. Jack Lemmon, the greatest. Over the years there were meetings with Edward G. Robinson, Harry Belafonte, Carroll O'Connor, Candace Bergen, Robert Taylor, June Allyson, Sarah Jessica Parker, and Roger Moore to name some. One was cynical and difficult. Another intellectual and shy. The rest, in no order, were remote, fun and playful, warm and charming, anecdotal and compassionate, insecure, an utter delight. I leave it to the reader to sort out which goes with whom.

Seated with Judy and others from the studio in the Bel Air's sumptuous dinning room, I waited for Lee Remick's arrival having not a clue what to expect, but doing a number on myself.

Would she talk to me, the writer, directly, or to me through the executives present. Would she even acknowledge my presence? Was she one of those who thought the writer was little more than an annoyance writing drivel that she and the director would have to sit up nights rewriting? Was it going to be Mitchum all over again?

Writers can do this to themselves.

No more than five minutes late, she strode in. Filled with high priced businessmen and travelers, the room went silent. Every eye was on her, and for good reason. She was a vision, elegant, gorgeous, captivating. Her persona, I would immediately learn, matched her appearance as she chose a seat next to me. Introductions made all around, the others at the table started in on a Hollywood ritual, the first name game.

"I was at Stanley's house last night."

"I must give Barbara a call."

"I hear Tom was at the Springs last weekend."

Lee, who'd not participated, smiled the game away, looked at me with her hand on my arm.

"And what magic are you going to weave for me?"

I've seldom been more motivated to accomplish a script as much as this one. I loved the story, about a genuinely heroic woman, nothing contrived, and I loved the actress I was going to be writing for. I virtually never have an actor or actress in mind when writing unless assigned to one. Some writers do. Some even have had their pictures on their bulletin boards above their then typewriters, now computers. I don't. This time I did, and it drove me.

I knew I was on tender ground with the love story. I could write it safely with a nod to George Bernard Shaw, whose male-female relationships were built on sexless, often intellectual conflicts. But this was Lee Remick. Lee Remick! Intelligent, intellectual, yes, but also very, very feminine, and alluring. There was no way I could not write the relationship with her Asian lover and eventual husband without infusing it with passion. Besides, it was their love story that drove them, threatened to derail them, reenergized them to complete their quest. I went for it. When the script was finished and sent to Lee I got a call.

"Thank you," she said. "Thank you."

The script went on to CBS. The following Monday I'd just settled in when Judy appeared in my doorway and gave me the news. CBS had turned it down. Both of us were stunned. I'd conned myself into thinking the quality of the story would overcome any misgivings the network might have about the relationship. No one at the network, when asked, would say why it was a no. I called Greg Mayday.

"What happened?"

"I'll tell you some day," he said.

His avoidance revealed the answer clearly. If it had been poorly written, or there was a problem with the construction or characters or dialogue or scenes, we'd have heard about it. It was the love story. And we knew it. America, in the network's eyes, then in the mid-1980s, was not ready to accept one of their iconic American beauties falling in love with, let alone marrying, an Asian. Not in TV land. Today? Less difficulty. But this was then. And it wasn't the only thing I'd come to care about that died. Soon thereafter so did Lee, taken by cancer. Of all the actors and actresses I've met I've wanted to write for, Lee Remick is the one lost opportunity I miss the most.

Just Remember, My Door Is Always Open

Sam Weisbord was holding court. Senior agent at the William Morris Agency, later to become its president, Chief Executive Officer and, finally, Chairman Emeritus, he'd represented, among others, Danny Thomas, Frank Sinatra, Elvis Pressley and Marilyn Monroe. He was telling me how he did it.

In negotiation with a studio or network head or representative, he'd always pick the hottest day.

"Come on, let's take a walk," he'd say.

Down El Camino Drive to Olympic, left toward Robertson, Sam would lay out the terms of the deal for his client. His opposite would invariably start out with a flat, "Ridiculous!" But the sun and his lack of conditioning would soon be getting to him. His luxurious designer suit would become stained with sweat. Sam, by contrast, in superb condition, was fully prepared to continue on to La Cienega till finally the deal he was offering began to sound better and better if only Sam would just turn back.

The several agents gathered in Sam's office to meet me, who'd heard this twenty times, broke into laughter. Having never heard it myself, I laughed too. Then Sam got down to it. I'd been called to William Morris because the agency wanted to sign me. I was the sort of client they wanted on their roster, he said, and the advantage would be mutual. The major agencies in town, he explained, CAA, ICM and William Morris, controlled the major talent, William Morris the leader among them, both motion pictures and television. The agency's record of packaged shows currently on the networks' schedules was unsurpassed. It was becoming more and more difficult, Sam went on, for independents to staff or cast their shows. By becoming a client of William Morris I would have access not only to their writers, directors and actors, but to the sales division of the agency. They were, in short, prepared to build me an empire.

The door opened, and Abe Lastfogel, then President of the agency, stuck his head in. It was clear he'd been asked to do so.

"Abe," Sam said with a burst of enthusiasm, "Meet the writer Chris Knopf. You know his work. He's seriously considering becoming a client."

Lastfogel shook my hand with a wan smile and it was clear he hadn't the vaguest idea who I was or what I'd written. A quick pretense of a business matter with Sam and Lastfogel was gone.

"So what do you think?" Sam asked.

I'd been represented by Bob Eisenbach for twenty-five years. While with the Frank Cooper Agency, Bob, then a literary agent with Cooper, was assigned to me, at the time a new client. A Stanford graduate, Bob, literate, fiercely loyal, provided more than the duties of an agent to me. He became a constant sounding board, making himself available any hour or day if I called. We became fast friends.

In the early 1960s Bob told me he was considering going off on his own, forming his own agency, and could do so if I'd go with him. I told him I would. Frank Cooper was angry. We'd had our differences over my contract at Four Star. Despite being told I would not sign a materials and packaging agreement which would allow the Cooper Agency a percentage of any show I created, he'd tried, unsuccessfully, to get it without my knowledge or approval. Still he was someone I genuinely liked, and would to this day. He sat me down and warned me I'd be making the mistake of my life, I'd be ruining my career. Bob Eisenbach, he insisted, was not a major player and never would be. I held fast, signed with Bob who soon formed what emerged as a highly respected boutique agency, Bob partnering with former writer-producer Harold Greene to form the Eisenbach-Greene Agency.

For two and a half decades our professional relationship and friendship grew as did my career, Bob tailoring it and nursing it.

"Be on notice . . . ." he'd call me, announcing an assignment I was being offered, or one he'd put me up for that had come through.

Our families met for dinners. I attended the wedding of his daughter, Barbara, to Kenny Heitz, starting guard on Lou Alcindor's undefeated UCLA national championship basketball teams.

Leave Bob for William Morris? I told Sam Weisbord that as flattering and attractive as the offer was, I simply couldn't do it. I'd be betraying a friend of too many years.

Sam looked at me, began nodding his head in admiration, turned to his colleagues in the room.

"In this town," he said, "in this day and time, have you ever heard such a thing? Something to remember, gentlemen, to take with you. A pure act of loyalty. So rare, I don't think I've ever heard it before." He turned to me. "This is not a wasted day. This is a memorable day. We're privileged to be part of it. Thank you."

I rose to leave, numb from all I'd just heard. Which was nothing to what he said next.

"Just remember, my door is always open."

As I walked across the street to the garage and my car I couldn't help realizing. That door, he hadn't closed it. And neither had I.

Two weeks later I stood in Bob's office and told him I was going with William Morris. Bob was stunned. I knew it was going to be crushing, I didn't realize how much. It must have been thirty seconds before he spoke.

"Why?"

I fell into a stream of consciousness repeating all I'd heard from Weisbord and how Boris Sagal the director and I had gone to CBS with an idea for a movie of the week which they turned down till we came back with Elizabeth Montgomery tied to the project and they'd said okay which proved the power of stars and William Morris had them...

I don't know if Bob heard what I had to say. His words, when he spoke, were monotone. He said he had my scripts, about fifty of them, he'd box them up and where did I want them sent?

I knew it was gong to be the toughest thing I'd ever do in my professional life. I didn't know it would be the worst. I deeply hurt a wonderful, decent man and close friend. Did I prosper from going to William Morris? I did well enough, probably no better than I would have had I stayed with Bob. I certainly lost the intimate association I'd had, the friendship and support. As for the empire William Morris was going to build for me, it took a while to realize, the agency was the empire. I was there to service it.

It was a year before Bob and I spoke again. He called me. Could we have lunch? We met at a small Italian deli on Santa Monica Blvd, just east of La Cienega. He wanted to know one thing. Was my leaving truly for my stated reasons, that William Morris could better my career? Or was it something else, something personal, maybe something he'd done or hadn't done that I hadn't told him. I assured him what I'd said was the reason, nothing more than that. He said he felt relieved to hear that, but I don't think he believed it. Of all the professional decisions I've ever made, it's the one I'd like to rescind. The one I can't forgive myself for.

The Battle For Linn Yan

"I'm dead! Finished! Done! My career's over!"

David Simons, in utter despair, was standing with me beside his Volvo on the 405 Freeway on the way to the airport, both of us staring at his flat.

I'd first met David in Judy Polone's office at ITC some months earlier. A bright, charismatic bundle of atomic energy, more than twenty years younger than I, he'd arrived with a concept of an unusual undercover detective series, entitled *Inside Straight*, blessed with a cast of off-center characters, most, I suspect, offshoots of himself.

I had never collaborated with anyone, but David wanted to learn about writing, and I wanted to learn production, which he intimately knew. We teamed, forming an entity, Knopf-Simons Productions, that would last ten years, eventually accounting for an Emmy nomination, two Writers Guild nominations, a People's Choice Award, an NAACP Image Award, an Entertainment Industry Council Special Commendation, a Christopher Award, and an Asian Pacific (AAPAA) Media Award.

Taking David's series concept to CBS, we got a script development deal, David and I writing the pilot script together which was eventually passed on by the network.

Series Pilots are a pain, a bastard form of writing, not necessarily to everyone, but to me, in which the writer must demonstrate how and where the characters and concept can evolve over four or five years. It's manufactured and open ended, which is not to my liking. The selection of which get shot, much less eventually make it to network schedules, is a complete crapshoot.

Witness how many do make it through the scheduling and testing process, highly thought of, hugely promoted, the guaranteed smash of the upcoming season, only to be cancelled within weeks for lack of an audience. Over the years I've been commissioned to write twenty-seven pilots. Seldom have I truly enjoyed the process, though fifteen of those I wrote were ordered to film, seven becoming series, a success rate, I'm told, considered high. My preference was always the self-contained story, and one of the best I ever experienced came immediately after *Inside Straight.* As usual it started with a phone call, and it came from David Simons.

"Your radio on?"

"No."

"Turn it on."

"What's happening?"

"Girl from Tennessee named Linn Yann just won the semifinals of the national spelling bee."

"Girls do those things."

"Four years ago she was in a death camp in Cambodia."

The story was an amazing one. It had, as David said, begun four years earlier. The Yann family's father had been killed, the mother and six children enduring a nightmarish existence facing ethnic genocide as Chinese Cambodians under domination of the brutal Khmer Rouge regime.

When the Vietnamese attacked Cambodia, Linn's mother,

Phoen, rescued her six children from the rice fields where the children had been put to work, forced to sleep on bare ground at night, escaping with them to Thailand in the confusion. There they were quartered in a refugee camp to either be sponsored out or sent back to Cambodia.

Hearing of their plight through a missionary speaking at their church in Chattanooga, Tennessee, George and Prissy Thrash, along with their teenage daughter, Laura, brought the entire family of seven, none of whom could speak a word of English, to America and into their home. Everything was foreign to them, even toilets, and especially the abundance of food which they took to hoarding under their beds.

Four years later Linn, by then fifteen, won the semi-finals of the National Spelling Bee. What happened in between we didn't know, but very much wanted to learn. There was a story there and both of us knew it. That it would end up becoming one of the most acrimonious, contentious projects I'd ever been involved in was at the time *not* known.

We took the concept to Judy Polone at ITC. Now elevated to the studio's second in command, Judy agreed to send David to meet with the Thrashes in Chattanooga to lock up the rights to Linn Yann's story if he could. We were not alone trying to do so. Lawyers and agents were calling the Thrashes on behalf of studios and clients. The calls came through while David was in their living rom. It was no contest. Charming, persuasive, David easily won over George and Prissy. It was presented to them that he, David, would produce and I would write. They asked to see a sample of my writing. I sent them the four hour CBS mini-series I'd written, *Peter and Paul,* and they signed with us.

A deal memo was drawn up quickly with CBS. Linn was to receive $5,000 as an option on her story, against a total of $50,000 if the film was shot, the money to be placed in trust for her college education, which provided a huge motive for David and me to make it happen. It was time for the two of us to return to Tennessee together, to get the full story, heading off in David's Volvo toward LAX, when there was that flat on the 405.

Planes flew everywhere and often in those days of the mid-1980s, so it was no difficulty getting a later flight to spend three days in Chattanooga with the Thrashes and Yanns. What emerged was far more than we'd anticipated.

From the day Linn arrived in Tennessee there was, in Prissy's words, "No child in her," so driven was she to succeed in all and everything she did. In school anything less than an A would send her diving under the table, curled into a fetal ball in silent hysterics. In sports she had to be the winner. Always. Entering the district, then state, then national spelling bee, her drive to win was desperate, confounding the Thrashes, till her back story began to emerge.

In the rice fields of Cambodia, Chinese-Cambodian children were worked to the bone. If any were found to be wanting, unable to do the work, became sick or too exhausted to go on, they were taken out and shot. Failure meant death, which was Linn's fear and driving motivation, her panicked need to forever succeed. How she would respond to eventually losing in the spelling bee, which she ultimately did, provided the suspense and drama of the story.

The script wrote quickly, David and I sitting across from each other day after day, loving the work. As stated, I was contracted to write it, David to produce it. When it was finished I paced my office for a day, called in my secretary, Dana, a wonderfully wise and supportive friend to both of us.

"I've got a problem," I said.

"Yes, you do."

"I can't leave David's name off this script."

"No, you can't."

Titled *The Girl Who Spelled Freedom*, it was turned over to Judy Polone, with the designated authorship, "Written by Christopher Knopf and David A Simons," on the title page. The following morning she called us into her office. She hated it! We were totally taken aback, so intense was her condemnation. Further at a 125 pages it was far too long. Of course it was long, it was a first draft. She didn't care, was in no mind or mood to listen to anything we had to say, or answer questions. She wasn't going to pay for it.

I called Bruce Brown, my agent at William Morris, who figuratively slammed a foot down on her neck. Relenting under threat from the Agency, she agreed to pay us for the draft as long as we got Bruce Brown off her back, none of which altered her opinion of what we'd written. She *hated* it! It had no heavies, no invention, we'd followed the facts too closely, it had no suspense, no arc to the story, totally was lacking what she called "High Concept."

"High Concept" was Judy's approach to story telling. It was a phrase of praise I'd heard her often use in validating material. Example. She'd told me once of an idea she'd taken to the network of a woman waking up one morning, turning to her husband, telling him how great he'd been making love to her during the night. The husband doesn't know what she's talking about, had slept straight through. A ghost, it seems, had come into the house and seduced her. That's the kind of story she liked and that's what she wanted and this sure in hell wasn't it!

David and I stared at each other, my blood pressure pushing 200, my pulse not far below. As for no heavy, I said, there *was* a heavy, a brutal one hovering over Linn, her terrifying fear of failure, of being destroyed by it. No invention? The story, the true story was loaded with invention, and drama, no need to embellish it. No suspense? It was filled with suspense, what was driving this girl, threatening to crush her if she could not overcome her past which was the arc of the story. Whatever we said, Judy held firm. She was not sending the script to the network.

"I can't accept this," I told her. "*I'm* taking it to the network."

"Go on, do it! They'll tell you the same thing!" she said.

That's not something you do, go over a studio executive's head. From this, as my sister would say, comes all kinds bad diseases. But I was livid. I sent the script to Gregg Mayday, the CBS program executive attached to the project. He called me the following day. He loved it.

Judy was neither persuaded nor mollified. A notes meeting was scheduled in Gregg's office at her request. Attending were David, me, Judy, her young male assistant and Gregg, who sat with the script in his lap. The one thing writers hate is to see their script in some authority's hands, page after page dog-eared, each representing a call for change. Gregg's script had about five. He went through them in ten minutes, most asking for a simple clarification or losing or adding a line. Finished, he turned the meeting over to Judy.

She opened her script. The corner of every other page, it seemed, was turned down. Angry black pencil lines were drawn across pages, accompanied by "No!"

What happened next I don't wish on anyone. Note after note that Judy presented was met by Gregg turning to David and me.

"What do you guys think?"

"We don't agree."

And Gregg turned back to Judy with, "Next note."

It went on for an hour and it was honestly painful. Over and over again the same thing, Judy presenting a criticism, Gregg turning to David and me, asking what we thought, we disagreeing, followed by Gregg turning back to Judy, asking for her next note.

Judy was not a trivial person. Starting as a low executive in my first meeting with her at ITC, she had worked her way up, doing so on her own, with drive and dedication, no one handing her anything. I'd always gotten along with her well out of mutual respect, and I'm still not sure I understand what soured her so. Her criticism seemed more personal than professional. Regardless, the meeting over, Gregg said he was sending *The Girl Who Spelled Freedom* on with his recommendation that it go to film. Harvey Shepherd, west coast head of CBS, turned it down as "too soft." To Judy's credit she did not chortle, though she did feel vindicated. It was a vindication that was short-lived.

Michael Eisner, newly appointed head of Disney Studios, was determined to restore the luster of the Disney name that had fallen into some disrepair. The most powerful way to do that, he reasoned, was to promote the brand to a mass audience by reviving the Disney franchise on prime time television. The idea of a weekly Disney show, a ninety-minute anthology, was presented to ABC and provoked interest. But what would be its signature, what would lead it off, thereby setting a tone for the show? From Eisner's book, *Work In Progress*, in part is the following.

"The first idea that caught on was a modern twist on the classic immigrant's tale. It was a true story about a mother and her children who make a harrowing escape from Cambodia during the Vietnam War. After hiding under their seats during their first airplane trip, they land in America. By the end of the movie not only are each of the kids excelling in school, but the oldest daughter, with all the drama of a Super Bowl victory, wins (sic) a national spelling bee. It was this story that I told over dinner the next week to Jane, Fred Pierce (Vice Chairman of Capital Cities-ABC) and his wife, Marion. When all four of us got tears in our eyes, I felt certain we should go forward. Not all our movies were equally stirring, but *The Girl Who Spelled Freedom* set an impressive standard."

The show was purchased by Disney to lead off for its new weekly anthology, brilliantly directed by Simon Wincer, starred Wayne Rogers and Mary Kay Place as George and Prissy Thrash. An unknown, Jade Chinn, played Linn. The show was called by critic Leonard Maltin "A delight", received multiple awards, among them an Emmy nomination. At the Television Academy dinner following the Emmy broadcast, Judy, looking smashing in a white evening gown, delightedly accepted congratulations from all around.

You've Got to Be
Willing to Point

In 1988, David Simons and I, under contract now to Orion Television, wrote and created a pilot for ABC entitled *Master Game* dealing with a CIA station agent working under cover as a mid-level functionary at the U.S. Embassy in Athens. The script did not make it to production, but was shown to Thomas Carter, one of the most sought after directors in television, as well as one of its most prominent African Americans. Thomas, who had a series development project with ABC, asked to meet. We did so, Thomas proving to be confident, poised, respectful, no sense he was sizing us up as he explained his concept.

Entitled *Equal Justice*, it would tell the personal and professional stories of a half dozen Assistant District Attorneys in the D.A.'s office of an unnamed northeastern city. It would call for gritty writing, mixed with humor and pathos. The pilot script would be two hours,   Thomas to direct and Executive Produce. David and I, approved by the network to write the pilot, would be Co-Executive Producers, credited along with Thomas for creating the series should it make the schedule.

I had never written anything dealing with the law. I had, in fact, after some seventy television scripts and eight produced motion picture screenplays, never written a courtroom scene. Enter Frank Ianucci.

A New York City Senior Assistant D.A. working out of the Bronx, Ianucci, who would later become the show's technical advisor, gave us the course. Trailing after him like interns after an acclaimed surgeon, we got a dose of his world that proved far different from what I'd anticipated. There was the judge, leaning back in his chair, seemingly engrossed in the proceedings, as he watched a baseball game on a small television set under his bench. There was the multi-millionaire defense attorney who turned up in court in a rumpled suit from Sears knowing a Bronx jury would not look sympathetically on a client represented by a lawyer in a silk Armani. There was the young Assistant D.A. who got caught taking a gun from the evidence room to impress a date he was trying to seduce. It was as much theater as law. As much gamesmanship as justice. And all about winning.

Another revelation was the age of most of the Assistant D.A.'s we met. Late twenties, early thirties. For a reason. A young lawyer fresh out of law school joining a firm will spend the first years of his or her employment, though well salaried, in the firm's library, researching cases. The D.A.'s office will put a brand new attorney to work from day one, admittedly at much lower pay, but offering nearly immediate courtroom opportunity, starting off with misdemeanors, the good ones rising rapidly to high profile felony cases.

A week with Frank Ianucci and we had our show. Format, characters, stories, style. The script, once written, was given an immediate go to production. Enter genuine madness. Casting.

Of all aspects of mounting a show, series or otherwise, casting has always proved the most debilitating. Not to me, but to actors who are handed what we call sides, a page or two of a scene, often uninformed about what's wanted, asked to read aloud before producers and directors, who, on rare occasion, have no clear idea of what they themselves are looking for.

Over the years I've seen some casting sessions handled beautifully, letting actors down gently, thanking them for coming in, acknowledging their talents, even applauding some role the actor's been seen in. Others have behaved less well, a director and producer once in my presence throwing a football around the room while an actor was being brought in to read.

Largely due to Thomas' reputation, things went smoothly as some high profile players were brought aboard. Jane Kazmarek as head of sex crimes. George DiCenzo, head D.A. Cotter Smith, number two man in the office, heading our unit of young Assistant D.A.'s, Sarah Jessica Parker, Barry Miller, Debrah Farentino, James Wilder. Which left two to be cast, one turning out to be an unintended but delightful twist, the other a mess.

Frank Ianucci simply had to be in our show. Not as an actor, but as a character. He was just too rich, too engaging and savvy to ignore. We portrayed him on paper much as he was. A senior D.A. of Italian origin who loved opera and liked to cook Italian sausages in his office in the morning for whomever might come by. Except. We couldn't find an actor of Italian heritage to play the role. One of the best actors available, known well to Thomas, was Joe Morton. Only Joe was Black. Joe was hired, no change in the character. The love of opera would stay, and so would the sausages.

The catastrophe was not of our making, but the network's. One of the richest roles in the script, at least to me, was patterned after a top felony prosecutor I'd encountered at the downtown Los Angeles Court House. A woman, early thirties, attractive, feminine, with a delightfully self-assured nature, she was a total transformation in court. Walking affably with me down the corridor, she strode into the courtroom with heel-clacking authority, came up against a young Latino accused of a brutal assault. Traditionally Latino men do not accept a woman holding authority over them. It was on his face, and on the faces of the several gang members present to support him. Eyes blazing, relentless, she pointed at him as she leveled the charges against him. I saw his smirk fold into a look of doubt as he searched the room for help that wasn't forthcoming. He cowered.

"You've got to be willing to point," she told me later. "Some can't do it."

Constantly courted to quit the DA's office for offers from prominent law firms in town at three times her salary, it became the importance of her work vs economic security. Which way to go?

I wrote her into the script, and gave her, all credit to Frank Ianucci's professional input, a dramatic closing argument in her felony case in the pilot. ABC told us not to bother casting the part. They knew who they wanted. An actress who'd had a minor role in a feature they'd seen. She was going to be a star, they said. We ran the picture. What ABC saw in her we couldn't decipher. Her performance was absent. We called her in for a reading of that closing argument. She came in stormy and agitated.

"This is terrible!" she said, waving the scene as she flopped into a chair. "This isn't real! This isn't dialogue!"

In fact she was afraid. And being afraid is the worst thing for an actor. Nervous, yes. Afraid, no. She got through the reading in an unsteady monotone, no sense of what was being asked of her, collapsed back in the chair when it was over, exhausted, overwhelmed. Nothing dissuaded the network to let us go in a different direction.

She was their choice, realizing too late their mistake when they saw the dailies. The shooting of the pilot completed, her part was cut to the bone and later completely eliminated from the series.

The other adventure in casting came later, in our second season. Thomas, and a director hired to shoot one of our episodes, got it in their minds to cast the role of a prostitute with the genuine article. Finding applicants wasn't a problem. Given our production location, a converted warehouse in a decrepit commercial area east of downtown Los Angeles, just open the door and beckon. A parade of scarlet sisters was run through the process. An exercise in futility. Not one of them acted like a hooker.

Returning to Los Angeles from filming the pilot in Pittsburgh, *Equal Justice* made the network schedule, with a limited order of twelve, to go on directly following the Academy Awards in early March, 1990. The show got outstanding reviews. It won the Peoples' Choice Award for the Best New Drama of the Year. Thomas twice won the Emmy for Best Direction Drama Series. Barry Miller, one of our cast, was nominated by the Golden Globes. The Casting Society of America gave it two nominations. What it did not get was ratings. At least not enough for ABC trying to build itself back into leadership over CBS and NBC. Later, ABC's Bob Iger, currently head of Disney, reportedly told Gary Randall, head of Orion Television, he thought they'd made a mistake cancelling the show. Which is what many cancelled shows often hear. Regardless, it was two years and out.

Also out were David and I. After a ten-year run, we were slowly dissolving our partnership. A tension had grown between us. And it had started before *Equal Justice*. We probably each have our own story to tell. For me, I'd begun to rankle at giving up my career-long identity as a writer to collaboration. My whole history till David and I formed our admittedly successful association had been my search for my own individuality. I stood or fell on it. And I missed it, returning to writing scripts for *Equal Justice* on my own. As for David, I suspect it was much the same, wanting, after ten years, his own place in the sun as well. We continued to work together in developing stories for the series, but separated as a writing team, David, at the close of the show moving into reality television, while I?

As usual, it came with a phone call.

Please, Don't Embarrass Us

"Ever hear of the Tuskegee Airmen?"

Thomas Carter was on the line. I'd heard of them. The all-Black fighter squadron of World War II.

"George Lucas has the rights to film their story." It was, I would learn, to be called *Red Tails*, after the red tailed P-51's they flew in Italy. "I'm to direct," Thomas explained.

"No kidding."

"He's got three scripts. None of them work. I need a rewrite."

"*George Lucas?*"

My sole experience with Thomas had been *Equal Justice*, but from the time I first met him, through development of the pilot and thereafter our two years on the series, I'd become genuinely fond of the man. Coming from humble origins, he'd gotten himself educated, truly educated, had entered the industry as an actor, eventually becoming a quadruple threat as actor-writer-director-producer. Three times winning an Emmy for his directing, three more times nominated, he was, with it all, consistently enthusiastic, courteous, a master at maintaining calm, and always on point. He was also dedicated, as I, to story, and the story he'd been handed to direct needed, he said, whole scale repairs.

"George Lucas doesn't know me from a hole in the wall," I said.

"You're approved."

No time to adjust to what I'd just heard, Thomas was going on. First I was to meet with them, the old Tuskegee fighter pilots. Three lived in the area. He'd set that up. Then read the scripts, then we'll talk.

I met with the three Tuskegee airmen, now elderly, all retired, in a hotel suite near the Los Angeles Airport. My first impression was there was a certain elegance and dignity to them all. College educated to a man, they greeted me pleasantly enough, but with a certain wariness I would not come to understand till later.

For the next two hours I listened, and what I heard were clearly the elements of an extraordinary tale. World War II was on the horizon and soon underway. Blacks, enlisted or drafted, were largely confined to mess halls and motor pools. Under the influence of Eleanor Roosevelt, an Air Corps program for training Black pilots was established at Tuskegee Air Field in Tuskegee, Alabama. It was a time when many in the military thought Black men lacked intelligence, skill and courage, concepts that many of their flight instructors subscribed to as well, early on washing out as many as they could get away with. Of the thirteen in that first class, only five made it through, to be eventually assigned beat up old P-40 rejects from Claire Chennault's China Command.

Prepared for war, under command of Captain, later Colonel, Benjamin O. Davis, a rare Black West Point Graduate, the all-Black squadron, the 99th as they were called, sat. Pilots and ground crews. No overseas orders. Maybe patrolling the coast for submarines, there was talk of that. But overseas combat? The first time they were jumped by a Messerschmitt, it was thought, they'd roll the plane over and hit the silk.

Finally orders came through. North Africa, the 99th Fighter Squadron to become part of the 33rd Fighter Group, which didn't want them. Sent to a make-shift isolated desert base dug out of a dry wash, they were assigned to strafing enemy trucks and ground troops across the Mediterranean in southern Sicily. But aerial combat? Forbidden. Even when Sicily was taken by the Allies and the 99th was transferred to the island did their orders remain firm. They were not to engage. Instead they were given "widow making" assignments, such as being ordered to fly night missions to protect parachute drops over eastern Sicily. The problem was at night there was no means of locating their base on return given the blackout condition and no directional signals to find it. The 99th's base commander refused to accept the assignment, saying it was a suicide mission.

The Air Corps had what it wanted, a direct refusal of orders. The 99th was grounded, the orders countermanded when Colonel Davis flew to Washington, met with the military high command, and made an impassioned appeal.

Still, they were in the war but not in it. Until jumped by German fighters one day while flying cover for American troops landing at Anzio. In aerial combat, they shot down six ME-109's. That got attention. And new planes. Red tailed P-51's. More than that it got the 99th a coveted assignment.

Bombers flying from Italy over the Alps to targets in southern Germany were being escorted by fighter planes. The problem was the white pilots, desperate for kills, were taking on German fighters in air-to-air combat, which left the bombers they were there to protect vulnerable to attack. The loss of bombers was intolerable. A change had to be made, and it was. The all-Black 99th Fighter

Squadron was assigned to fly cover. Which it did, no one ever deserting the mission, and never losing a single bomber under the 99th Fighter Squadron's protection to enemy aircraft for the rest of the war.

I'd heard snippets and rumors of the 99th and its exploits over the years, especially when I was in the Air Corps myself, but never from the men who'd been there. Told straightforwardly by these three, without theatrics, it was theatrical as hell. An incredible story of overcoming not only prejudice, but fear, both through performance. For me it was themes I hadn't been able to delve into since before *Equal Justice* which had been mostly accommodation writing, tailoring stories to our various characters, but little for me in the process. This would be writing from the gut again. As I thanked them and turned to leave, one addressed me at the door.

"Please," he said, "don't embarrass us."

I had no idea what he was talking about till I read the three scripts Thomas had sent me. They were basically the same, telling the general outline of what had occurred, but almost, it seemed, serio-comedy. No criticism of the writers who apparently had done what was asked. But the style and form in which the story was told, almost satirical it seemed to me, full of high jinx and tomfoolery, made no sense to me whatsoever.

"Don't embarrass us," the old pilot had said.

Now I understood what he was talking about. The approach taken in these scripts embarrassed them totally. Me as well.

I met Thomas at his office on the Columbia lot and we walked, first stop being the incredible set being prepared for Spielberg's *Jurassic Park*. Getting down to it, I told him my excitement about all I'd heard from the airmen, but my bewildered reactions to what

I'd read. How did Lucas see this? It seemed as though I'd encountered two separate stories, the true one I'd heard from the airmen, the other distorted and mostly fictional. Thomas agreed. I asked him what he wanted me to do. Break down the story as you know it, he told me, then we'd meet with Lucas at his northern California facility, Skywalker Ranch.

I was dubious. "Based on the three scripts I read, he's not going to go for this."

"Just give me what I want," Thomas answered, "and we've got a movie."

George Lucas

George Lucas' Skywalker Ranch is located off a secluded but open country road in Marin County north of San Francisco. Turning in at a modest gate late in the day after a flight from Los Angeles, I was greeted by guards who verified my name on a visitor's sheet, politely cautioned me, no pictures, and directed me to a large two-story house just off the entrance for visitors spending the night. A room was waiting for me. Dinner, if I wanted it, could be found back out to the road, a mile further west to a small but recommended country restaurant. Please, I was told, keep all receipts for reimbursement. Fruit, cereal, toast and coffee could be found in the kitchen in the morning for breakfast, self-served. There was a full library of books and tapes of motion pictures for my use if I wished. My meeting with Mr. Lucas and Mr. Carter was at ten the next day in Mr. Lucas' office, in the main building up the road at the far end of the ranch.

At a quarter to ten the following morning I was in my airport rental and heading up. I've always loved California's natural beauty, and this, its meadows and rolling hills, was among the best of it. Assembled parcel by parcel since 1978 fifteen years earlier, the ranch's 4,700 acres, only fifteen under development, cost Lucas, by most estimates, $100 million. There was a barn with animals, vineyards, a garden with vegetables and fruits that served the kitchens. There was a man-made lake, an observatory, a three hundred-seat theater, multiple screening rooms, as well as the ranch's own fire station.

To the left as I drove was what appeared to be a winery, which, in fact, was no winery at all, but a facility for post production. The main house at the end of the road, a genuinely beautiful structure, appeared to be a replica of an immense Victorian. It was home to Lucas' executive offices. Entering, a grand staircase curved to the second floor. As directed, I took it, and arrived at Lucas' complex. A moment later and I was ushered into his office.

The first thing I noticed was the office itself. It was comfortable and unpretentious, as was Lucas when I met him. Seated across from Thomas who was already there, Lucas rose to greet me. Dressed in work shirt and jeans, there was, I felt, a reserve about him. Not diffidence, but not shyness either. He seemed somewhat scholarly, which gave me the impression I was coming into a professor's office to be assessed for a grade.

Amenities over—how was the flight, how was my room, and the restaurant?—we got down to why I was there. Had I read the scripts? What did I want to change?

The question threw me, the inference being Lucas basically had what he wanted, was amenable to improvement, but change? Not a whole lot expected. And change was what I had in mind. I glanced at Thomas. He looked confident. His look said, "Go for it." So I did.

There were two separate, very different openings to the screenplay I'd thought of, I told Lucas. The first, a prologue to the film, would feature the introduction of one of the two leads, the younger, less sophisticated of the two, Joe Callender, picking him up as a young boy, about ten, a Black child living with his parents in a nearly all white community at the edge of a small town airport in the upper Midwest. The boy, obsessed with planes and flight, against his father's orders, constantly headed to the hangars where planes were being serviced, generally making a nuisance of himself as he begged for all the information he could get from white mechanics and pilots.

Though more in keeping with the tone of Lucas' three scripts, I told him I rejected this opening out of hand. I knew it had a certain "smile" to it, would be an audience pleaser, but aside from the fact it was cliché and ordinary, it established only that the boy wanted to fly. That was not the theme of the story which was the prejudice toward *any* Black thinking he had a chance in hell of becoming a flight officer in the United States Air Corps, especially during war. I outlined to Lucas the second scene I had in mind, the one I wanted. In fact, I'd already written it.

FADE IN:

INT. CALLENDER APARTTMENT
– DARKNESS

An alarm clock clangs in the dark. A bed spring creaks. A man's voice calls out.

ANGUS' VOICE

Shut that damn thing off!

A grunt sounds above the tinny ring of metal. Bare feet pad across the floor and the clang ceases abruptly. Light floods the curtained alcove, reveals JOE CALLENDER. Twenty, Black, naked. A pretty boy who thinks he knows how to use it. Smart, stubborn, driven, lots to prove and get away from. He's straightened his hair. It tells us something.

INT. CALLENDER APARTMENT – EARLY DAY

A well-thumbed copy of LIFE MAGAZINE, March 24, 1942, is laid out on the room's chipped wooden table. Five military aviators are pictured, the first Air Corps class of Black flyers to graduate from Tuskegee. A caption spells it out. Joe's locked on it, though he's seen that picture a thousand times. Dressed now, he wears a cheap suit, cheaper shirt and tie.

The apartment, we see, is one room. Meager furnishings. The curtain, now drawn back, separates Joe's sleeping area. Breakfast odors drift from behind as ADA CALLENDER, Joe's mother approaches from the two burner stove with a plate of crinkled bacon and a pot of coffee.

A long-suffering woman she has never known a better life, wears an old cotton robe, and a cross. Joe is a wonder to her. Joe who has gotten himself educated, who has beat the streets. Joe whom she worships. She takes his hand.

ADA

Lord, we thank you for the food and protecting our souls and wish Joey safety...

ANGUS

Nigger, you crazy!

And the magazine is suddenly pulled out from under Joe.

ANGUS CALLENDER has crossed from the bed he shares with Ada. Joe's father, he wears coveralls, no shirt, is barefoot. A deep, choking self-hatred and failure has become his life. He no longer understands hope, resents it in his son. A pint of rum bulges from his hip pocket. Glancing at the picture of the Black flyers, he drops it contemptuously back onto the table.

ANGUS

All they want a Black man for's dig ditches.

ADA

(to Joe) You want me to pour some coffee for you?

ANGUS

Oh, tha's right. (as she pours Joe's coffee) Boy here's special. Gone an' got hisself some college.

He bangs an empty cup on the table, demanding she pour him coffee, too, as he holds his free hand to his mouth and ear, mocking a phone call.

ANGUS

Mistuh Roosevelt, suh? They raisin' some sand over there in Germany, an' boy here say you looking' for college niggers...

ADA

Don't profane.

ANGUS

Shut your mouth! One fool in this family's enough!

JOE

Don't tell her to shut her mouth!

ANGUS

Gimme that skillet, woman..!

ADA

Lord! Lord..!

Joe pushes from the table, moves to his bed, lifts his cardboard suitcase, straps it. Angus shakily pours rum into his coffee.

ANGUS

Nigger, you makin' the mistake o' your life.

ADA

(heading Joe out) You got your papers, Joey, your ticket...

Joe ignores his father, though his eyes are ablaze.

ANGUS

Every honky you meet'll have it in for you! You gonna know it!

ADA

Angus, he did this, he got there! He wants you proud..!

JOE	(grabs suit case and folder) I don't want his praise.
ANGUS	They ain' goin' to let you make it, if that don' scare you. You make it they ain' goin' let you mean anything.
JOE	The only thing scares me is ending up like you. That scares the hell out of me.
ANGUS	Get him out!
JOE	(to his mother) I'll write, I'll send money...
ANGUS	The bastard, get him out!
	Joe kisses his mother goodbye. She wants to clutch him. He heads toward the door.
ANGUS	The eight ball's at the end o' that dream you travellin'! You always be a nigger an' don' forget it!

A perfect scene? Not by a long shot. Clearly open to revision. But the sort of scene I felt was needed to set up one of the two lead characters and what was at stake. Particularly as the sequence to follow, Joe's arrival along with others at the Tuskegee air base, was to be filled with humor and nervous chatter and tension as the men first encounter each other, and witness a sudden, unexpected dramatic, near-tragic occurrence.

Lucas was unresponsive which I took to mean what he'd heard was not what he'd hoped for nor wanted. In his lap were three type-written pages. His fingers were running down them, an outline, I assumed, of how he wanted the movie to go.

So went the morning, Lucas listening intently, saying little or nothing as I presented the revised characters and approach to the first half of the movie which I'd worked out in detail. And over and over those three pages, his fingers running down them as I spoke.

Lunch was more convivial. Taking us to the building's cafeteria, it was clear from the moment we entered George Lucas was revered. Not barging the food line, but settling in at the end of it, his relationship with one and all seemed casual, open and friendly. I hadn't seen anything quite like it since my days at Four Star with Dick Powell. Here was one of the entertainment industry's most illustrious figures and no one, but no one in that room, seemed inhibited.

I was beginning to feel *who was I to disagree with him*, given his incredible prominence and reign of success. But I didn't know how to do anything other than what I believed, the way I saw the story, which was the way it happened. Returning to Lucas' office I soldiered on with my approach to the second half of the movie, bringing in humor where it belonged along with the drama, Lucas continuing to run his fingers down those three pages. When I was finished, I could see he was not happy. I asked him, given that it was his show, how *he* saw this picture.

"I see it as a celebration of flight," he said.

Whatever answer I anticipated, that wasn't it. *A celebration of flight?*

"George," I said, genuinely baffled, "this is a story about being subjected to, battling, and overcoming prejudice. That's what it's *always* been. That's what the Tuskegee airmen I met in Los Angeles expect it to be."

He answered calmly. "I'm not going to put $20 million into a movie that's going to get a lot of awards and no one's going to go see."

That night Thomas and I drove into San Francisco for dinner at Postrio's on Post Street. Over dinner we talked. I had a firm commitment, pay or play, to deliver a screenplay, but what was I to write? Thomas was unperturbed. He endorsed my approach, told me to go with it, felt confident Lucas could be brought around.

Three months later I delivered my script to Thomas.

"Now," he said, "I've got something to work with."

Lucas didn't agree. He turned the script down, and Thomas with it. I wrote Lucas a note, thanking him for the assignment and the opportunity to meet him, but pleading the airmen's case not to embarrass them. I never got a reply.

And, oh, those three pages Lucas kept referring to as I took him through my approach to the story? During the afternoon session he got up, left the room for a moment. I chanced a glance at the pages. They were not an outline of how he saw the story as I supposed. Listed on the three pages were the 100 most successful movies of all time.

The Meanest Divorce

"From a point of prestige, they're important to us. But our accounting department keeps telling me they're a waste, to stop making them. Too expensive, market's saturated, they're a financial loser."

It was Les Moonves, President, CBS Entertainment. I was a member of the Writers Guild Committee on Television Long Form (Movies for TV) and we were meeting with the industry's CEO's at the Beverly Hills Hotel. We'd occasionally done so in the past, mostly to discuss such matters as late pay and excessive rewrites. Now we were facing something else. MOW's were still a network staple, sort of, and, throughout the 1970s and 1980s, also were mine. Two hours, three hours, mini-series. I'd written a dozen, all filmed except that one for Lee Remick, seven achieving award recognition.

If it was a warning, I didn't take it seriously, no need to, as I was in the midst of writing a television movie for CBS. I loved the form. And why not? I was on everyone's so called "A" list, picked the projects I wanted to do, and generally, with that one exception, *Escape From Bogen County*, was encouraged to do them as I saw them. Further I'd managed to find outstanding, contributing producers to work with who did their all to help me achieve what I wanted to do.

Among the best had been Beth Polson who had an incredible talent for getting her projects into production. Four times nominated for an Emmy, winning once for producing the Barbara Walters Specials, Beth went off on her own in the 1980s with the intent to produce movies for television. I was the first writer she hired. The script, entitled *Not My Kid*, from an idea by Beth, was based on an actual drug rehab center in St Petersburg, Florida. Kids on drugs were placed, some by their parents, some by court order, to be rehabilitated by other kids who'd been on drugs themselves and had become clean, "Get honest" being the mantra heard over and over from the staff.

It was a controversial and contested concept. At first I turned it down, for reasons to be learned in the final chapter of this book. But a self-realization, also dealt with later, turned me around. It would portray a father who discovers his teenage child is deep into drugs and, in all ignorance, decides he's going to handle it himself. Starring Stockard Channing and George Segal as the parents, the resultant script, for Marian Brayton's CBS Specials, won both a Humanitas and Writers Guild nomination.

The second for Beth, *Baby Girl Scott*, also for CBS Specials, was equally controversial, dealing with the impotence families can suffer over the fate of terribly premature newborns. Hospitals and ethics committees having, at that time at least, the ultimate authority to determine their fate, often meant parents, with no say at all, suffered through the agony of efforts to save their newborns even when they were beyond saving. It was something, again, I'd gone through myself. Taking the side of the parents in the film, starring John Lithgow and Mary Beth Hurt, it was again contentious, flying in the face, as it did, of the medical establishment.

These had been terrific projects to work on, personal, even cathartic, Beth driving me to explore and achieve both as best I could, never settling for less. She could do that and did, supported by Marian Brayton at CBS who got both into production as written, controversies and all.

Now there was this new project at CBS, thankfully more of the same, that would, of course, be treated the same. Oh, really? If I'd only read the tea leaves.

It was a true story, from an article written by Skip Hollandsworth for the October, 1992 issue of *Texas Monthly*, entitled *The Meanest Divorce*. In 1984, while divorcing his wife, Carolyn, Chuck Smith, then twenty-six years old, the scion of one of Houston's wealthiest and most politically influential automobile dealers, kidnapped his own two sons, aged six and four, and vanished for more than seven years. Later Chuck would testify that the boys tearfully begged him to take them away from their mother, who had become so addicted to prescription drugs that she slept through the day, forgetting to feed them, shaking them when they awoke her. The tabloids, covering the story, read, "He kidnapped their kids. She bankrupted his family. He hid for seven years. She had him put in jail. A story of love turned to hate."

I flew to Houston to get Carolyn Smith's side of the story. Meeting her in her modest one-story home, her lawyer present, I learned Carolyn, as a simple, relatively uneducated, but very attractive girl had been swept off her feet by Chuck Smith, considered by most I spoke to as the black sheep of the family. His parents had objected fiercely to his marrying Carolyn, and treated her like poor trash throughout their marriage. Unable to cope she turned to drugs. Following the kids kidnapping she got herself well, used every resource available to her to find and reclaim her children, who'd been consistently bombarded by the Smiths with horrible tales of their mother, so much so they came to believe them. So even though she eventually reclaimed the boys through the courts, she then had the battle of reclaiming their trust and love.

It was a hell of a story. A woman overwhelmed by low self-image and failure finding strength and courage to fight immense odds and prevailing. It was home territory for me. The script wrote easily and was turned in to the head of Long Form Development at CBS who told us it was a go to production subject to acceptable casting.

It was all up to the producer now, the very accomplished Diana Kerew. As for me, another project had come my way. Pat Finnegan, who with her husband Bill had founded one of the most successful independent production companies in town, Finnegan Associates, had a concept for a television movie. Buy a gun out of fear, you'll use it out of fear. Joanna Kerns, a wonderful actress, sister to Donna DiVerona, Olympic gold medalist swimmer, was attached to it. So was NBC.

I'd not only worked for the Finnegans in the past, they were close personal friends. Lorraine and I had travelled to France with them, twice, putted along the Canal du Midi with them, crewed for them on their ketch in the Mediterranean. Pat was a perpetual delight, and so was Joanna from our initial meeting. I'd hear from Diana Kerew when there was something to hear. It wasn't long in coming.

As happened with *Escape From Bogen County* and *Scott Joplin* before it, a new Head of Long Form had turned up on the scene replacing the old, trashing nearly everything he inherited that was in development at the network. Mine was to be preserved. Conditionally. A rewrite was called for, a heavy one. To hell with what really happened, we were told. Just use it as a template.

But a template for what? Nobody seemed to know why this was being asked for, but I did. Once while touring Africa we were following a leopard, watching it urinate on African tulip trees every fifty yards or so.

"What's he doing?" I asked our guide.

"Establishing his territory."

The Meanest Divorce, as it was called, was a wonderful story, a true one, the network originally, and I thoroughly, having committed to telling it as it happened. With no Berry Gordy to fight for the project, as he had done with *Scott Joplin*, I asked for a meeting with the new Head Of Development which was refused, told to go through the Program Executive assigned to the show whose job was to accomplish his boss's bidding. I turned down the rewrite, incurring acrimonious response from all around for doing so, and moved on to the project for Pat Finnegan and Joanna Kerns.

The premise was a simple one. A woman, to be played by Joanna, is on jury duty, the defendant a gang kid. His fellow gang members, seated in the courtroom, pick out Joanna as the most easily intimidated among the jurists, do so with threatening looks throughout the trial. Out of fear she tries to hold out for acquittal in the jury room, finally is overwhelmed by the others, votes for conviction. Terrified that she's marked for retribution, which she is not, she buys a gun, knowing nothing about its use, which ultimately leads to an unnecessary and tragic result.

The network, upon hearing the story, ordered the script without comment. Completed, Joanna told me it was the best she'd had written for her. It was turned in to the network, Joanna and I called to a meeting.

As we entered, it was clear something was wrong. There was a tension in the department. A sort of scattered confusion. It seemed to be everywhere. As for the script, no, no, it was not what they wanted, not at all! Our entire approach to the story was wrong! She should have been harassed and threatened after the trial by the gang, and no one would listen to her, no one would believe her, so buying the gun for protection, she takes on the gang heroically, all by herself. Another story entirely. A safe and usual one. Nothing wrong with it, but not the one we'd sat for an hour telling them we were going to write.

What had happened was clear enough. At least I thought it was clear and hold to that thought to this day. The market on movies made for television, "Made For" as they were euphemistically called, was shrinking, and so was its audience. The days of examination of the human condition, its failures and foibles, and therefore oneself, were going if not gone. At least on network television which had a mass audience to appeal to in order to survive. And that beast, hungry for the familiar, must be fed. Les Moonves had given clear warning. And I hadn't listened.

Streptococcus Viridins Endocarditis

"Call your doctor."

"I will."

"Now."

"Soon as I'm home."

"No, you call him now!"

I was in an acupuncturist's office, Dennis Kessler, to whom I and Lorraine had periodically gone over the years.

For the past three or four weeks I'd been going through something I'd never experienced. Surging temperature, sweating, shivering, loss of appetite and weight, and an almost crippling pain in my lower back. I assumed it was a flu of some sort, but that pain in my back was a killer. Having had luck with Dennis Kessler's acupuncture in the past, I went to him.

"This isn't something for me," he said, "This is something else."

I called my doctor while still in Dennis' office, was told to come over. One look at me and he said, "How would you like to go to the hospital." It wasn't a question.

Admitted to Cedars Sinai, tests were run, and I was hurriedly transferred to the cardiac unit. Some weeks before I'd had my teeth cleaned. Having a mitral valve prolapse, i.e. a leaky heart valve, an antibiotic, Amoxicillin, is always to be taken before any dental or other invasive procedure. I knew this, had been doing so religiously for several years since first being diagnosed. Except this once. I'd forgotten. Result? I was infected with streptococcus viridins endo-carditis. Without immediate treatment death follows.

Treatment was immediate, fourteen days in the hospital with masses of intravenous antibiotics, then home for further antibiotics administered by a battery operated pump strapped to my side. For six more weeks I wore a permanent intravenous line, Lorraine daily changing the medication. The infection overcome, I was turned over to surgeons to repair the damaged valve, which they did, inserting an annuloplasty ring around it which saved the valve and has served me well for the past fifteen years.

The second hospital stay for surgery was eight days. My friend, Dick Simmons, who'd gone through open heart surgery himself, had told me "It's not as bad as you think." He was right. And it wasn't without some perverse pleasures. Walking up and down the corridors, as I'd been instructed to do, pushing my intravenous monkey bar ahead of me, I took delight in the glares of other cardiac patients too lazy or stubborn to get out of their beds and do the same. Further, one of the patients was a screamer, demanding constant attention, which abounded to my benefit, as the nurses, fed up with him, hid out in my room as I regaled them with all the important stars I'd worked with. Till I realized. This was Cedars. All the important stars came here. They'd probably met more than I had.

With it all, I couldn't escape a gnawing, nagging feeling. I was approaching seventy. What writers were still being hired around that age? Frank Pierson and Bob Towne. And fast coming on was the culture of youth, advertisers, studios and networks slanting the writing of their shows and movies more and more by and for the young whose patterns of buying were not solidified, who paid money to go to the movies instead of waiting to rent cassettes or see them on late night television. There was a new day dawning, and it was gray.

Eulogist To the Stars

Stage two, "Get me Chris Knopf." Stage five, "Who's Chris Knopf?"

The new century had dawned, and I, after nearly fifty years, forty in stage two, found myself clinging to it by my fingernails. I'd always admired Sandy Koufax of the Los Angeles Dodgers going out on the top of his game. If it was good enough for Sandy it was good enough for me. I did the same. Ended it before being dropped unceremoniously into stage five, took my pension, Lorraine and I variously escorting one or more our nine grandchildren or just ourselves to skin and scuba diving off the Galapagos Islands, outracing an elephant in Africa, descending into tombs in Egypt, staring down cobras in Morocco, navigating the canals of southern France, sailing the Mediterranean in Bill and Pat Finnegan's fifty foot ketch, ballooning in Burgundy, Lorraine getting her virginity back in the mystical waters of Delphi, losing it again that night.

Except it didn't end that way. For reasons still foreign to me, I became the eulogist to the stars. Not the ones on Hollywood's Walk Of Fame, though one did make it, but the writers who'd been luminaries in my life. Ellis Marcus, Sy Salkowitz, David Humphrey Miller, Albert Aley, Sam Rolfe, George Kirgo, Ray Goldstone, Father Elwood Kaiser, Richard Alan Simmons, Gene Roddenberry.

It's a funny thing about eulogies. The best are memorable

when the subjects are memorable, and all of these writers were. All people I'd grown up with and worked with in this industry, some with greater or lesser reputations than others, but friends, supportive of each other, hiring and working for each other, now gone. Over the years I've been asked to memorialize them, or share in the effort. From Sy Salkowitz and Father Kaiser going out with cancer, to Ellis Marcus and Dick Simmons, heart, to Sam Rolfe going for an overhead lob on his tennis court, never coming out of it, to Gene Roddenberry.

Gene did not go well or easily. He had diabetes and wouldn't obey the rules. He was at Sam Rolfe's house one night, a dinner party. I asked Majel, his wife, how he was doing. She answered, and she was angry.

"Badly. And he's not going to get better."

Gene had always been one given to the free play of passions, and was overt about it. "A man lives his life as it happens," he once said, "Or he turns his back on it and withers away." World War II bomber pilot, Pan American pilot who crash landed in Arabia, cop, Gene was anything but withering, but his excesses were catching up to him. It was two weeks after Sam Rolfe's party that Sam and I visited Gene for lunch at his Bel Air mansion. Few things carry more pain, disturb more, than watching a great man lessened. It was the last time we ever saw him, though he tried to appear that he was improving. He wasn't, starting a sentence then faltering, no idea where the thought was supposed to go. I'd lived through that with my father.

Three of us were asked to speak at his funeral service. Ray Bradbury, the actor, Patrick Stewart, and I. The auditorium was packed. A squadron of planes flew by overhead in respect, the traditional one plane missing in salute.

Star Trek, of course, as well as Gene was on everyone's mind. It *was* Gene. A NASA space ship had been named after his star ship *Enterprise*. His ashes would later be sent by rocket into space. I doubt I was the first to hear about the birth of *Star Trek*. But the day I did was in front of 50,000 people, as I told the gathering at Gene's funeral.

It was a day almost thirty years earlier when I found myself with a pair of tickets you don't often get. Dodger stadium, right behind home plate.

"Can MGM live without you for an afternoon," I asked Gene.

"Absolutely not," he answered. But there we sat, four hours later, Gene and I, in our two choice seats, and it was late in the game which was close.

"Do you want to hear an idea?" he asked.

"No," I told him, which never stopped him and didn't then, as Johnny Roseboro of the Dodgers edged off third.

It was for a new series, about an airship, a dirigible, in the late nineteenth century. A multi-racial crew of men and women, traveling the skies to still uncharted, unknown places, encompassing our own failures, yearnings, lusts, confusions, aspirations, fears and furies, yet with it all trying to bring decency and equality to a world grown hostile from ignorance and suspicion.

Was it the beginning of something that a few years later was to capture everyone's imagination? I didn't know. Many of us, I'm sure, can lay claim to be in on that birth. But it captivated me, and for one brief instant fifty thousand people, it seemed, who rose in a great roar of approval. For Gene? Soon enough but not yet. Johnny Roseboro had stolen home, and neither one of us had seen it.

MVP

The alarm rang. I caught it quickly. It was five in the morning, December 20, 2007, my birthday. When I was seven years old, tossing at night, worrying about death, it was an age I never thought I'd see. I was eighty.

Slipping out of bed, I looked across in the dark at Lorraine. She was still sleeping, beautiful even in sleep. *How does she do it? One of life's mysteries.* I shaved, didn't shower, I'd do that when I got back, stepped into my jeans, left the house and got into my car. It was freezing, though I'd dressed for it. The temperature gauge on the dash read 43°.

Twenty minutes later I turned into the Veterans Memorial Park parking lot off Culver Blvd. There were already a dozen cars there and others arriving. Getting out, I crossed Overland to the long familiar walls once encasing MGM Studios. Now it was Sony, and the lion was gone. Up Overland to just before the studio entrance where a table had already been set up with juices, coffee and doughnuts. Somebody had brought homemade muffins. Nodding to others already arriving, I picked a sign off the stack against the wall, walked up to Washington Blvd, turned right to the first delivery gate, took up my accustomed position pacing back and forth across the entrance, sign held high. It was six o'clock in the morning, the sky just beginning to turn. The Writers Guild was on strike.

It wasn't long before the rest of the writers assigned to this shift at this post, from six to ten in the morning, would arrive. There was Christopher Dunn, Gigi McCreery, far younger writers, both with young children to support, both of whom had walked off secure employment in support of the cause.

The three of us sort of became a trio, I regaling them about the early years, they telling me of how it had all changed. Others arrived, picket signs in hand. Some I knew, some I didn't but would get to know. Some wrote for television, others for movies, some for both. Still more were showrunners, creators of their own on air series, and all had put down their pens, and not a complaint about it from anyone. Histories were shared and bonds were formed, writers who'd heard about each other, but had never met.

"*You* wrote that? No kidding. Loved it!" was heard more than once.

With the emergence of daylight Sony employees began to arrive, one always energizing our day, an anonymous studio exec in suit and tie, roaring by in his BMW on his way in, contemptuously giving us the finger. He was no match for the blaring horns in support of us from cars passing by. We began to keep count. Most came from mid sized vehicles, pick ups and trucks, and Priuses for some reason, always Priuses, even a city bus driver or two, and, if you can believe, even once a Sony ten-wheeler turning into the gate giving us horn and a high five. We had the sense we were walking the pavement for more than just us, figuratively going up against the same forces that controlled *their* lives.

It was the first time since the sixties writers had been this unified as throughout the town, at Sony, Fox, Warners, Disney, Paramount, Universal, Columbia, NBC, ABC, CBS writers gathered daily by the thousands, regardless of weather, six in the morning till dark, in support of the Guild and its demands.

What did we want? In a word, jurisdiction over new Media that we didn't have, that had been refused us since the 1980s. Over twenty years the studios had been telling us they would give us our fair share of residuals and reuse payments once any new market developed. Animation, cable shows, the internet, DVD's. Now that the new markets were here, the studios demanded that we choose between a meaningless "study" of New Media or gut our livelihood through profit based residuals. *Profit* based? In the 1960s I'd been hired to write a pilot for Screen Gems, a subsidiary of Columbia Studios. In negotiations I was to receive a traditional royalty for each episode produced should the pilot make it to series. I was also to be given five percent of the producer's profits.

"Tell you what I'll do," I countered. "You keep your five percent and give me just a hundred dollars more each episode."

Their response? "That's not fair!"

The point? Anytime we're offered a percentage of profits, all subject to their creative accounting, we won't receive enough to buy a frame for the check. In short, what the studios were trying to do, having always hated the concept of rerun payments, was to ensure that any new medium would not encumber them with that burden.

Why rerun payments at all? I'm forever asked. If a man sells a dining room table should he be paid a further payment every time someone sits down to eat at it?

In the 1950s the industry rule of thumb was that the writing budget of a movie was five percent of the cost of the film. Today, taking an MOW for example, much less a motion picture, the writing budget is closer to two percent. Often less. As such, as we properly see it, the money a writer gets to write his or her script is a down payment against the success of a show, which, *if* successful, will be rerun accordingly, the writer to receive additional payment the more it's performed. Not much different than a writer of a novel, given an advance upon sale, plus royalty payments if the book sells well, little or nothing more if it doesn't. The same for a theatrical play. If it folds out of town, the writer's billfold remains pretty bare. If it goes to New York and becomes a hit, the writer profits. As with composers, the artist receiving royalties off the sale of his or her CD's, the amount depending upon their success. As for writers of motion pictures and television, months, even years between sales can be lean, their sole means of support often coming from reuse payments for work previously produced. That parking lot in the Veterans Memorial Park off Culver Blvd was not filled with Mercedes and BMWs.

The sun was up higher now, the temperature into the fifties, when word was passed along the line that at the end of this shift, at ten, there would be a gathering at the Overland entrance to the Sony lot. Luvh Rakhe, our lot chairman, had something to tell us. Someone, I think it was Chris Dunn, said he had to leave early, and took off.

At ten o'clock, foot sore, we headed back to the Overland entrance. A large group had already gathered, the Sony lot having seven entrances, each with its separate assignment of picketers. Luvh had one of those hand held electronic megaphones. Climbing up on a small mound of grass he addressed us.

"We have an MVP among us," he began. I don't remember the rest that he said, but when he was finished out came a huge three-foot by two-foot birthday card, signed by dozens of writers who'd been on the shift. "Thanks for everything," one said. "Thanks for the residuals." "You walk, you rock!" "Don't go changin'" "Many, many years!"

That wasn't all. There was Chris Dunn moving out of the crowd with the largest birthday cake I'd ever seen.

When my father died, my mother asked me, didn't I want my father's scripts? He'd had them all bound, all thirty odd movies he'd produced, in red engraved leather with embossed gold lettering. In all honesty, they were the last thing I wanted, not out of disrespect, but what was I going to do with them? Store them in a box in the garage, too guilty to throw them away? I suggested maybe a university might like them which she thought was a good idea and sent them off to one.

Because of this I'd trashed almost all of my own scripts, about eighty of them, kept maybe ten, not wanting to pass the same guilt trip on to my kids who'd really, honestly have no use for them. I did the same with my awards, for the same reason, keeping just two. One is the Christopher Award I'd received for the Disney MOW, *The Girl Who Spelled Freedom*, given to "a writer who affirms the highest value of the human spirit." The other is that birthday card.

Millard Kaufman

It was a spring day four years ago. Millard Kaufman was on the phone.

"Listen, sorry, I'm not going to be able to make lunch this week."

Lunch was a floating affair that's been going on for years. Milliard, I, Stan Kallis, director and former President of the Motion Picture Academy Arthur Hiller, Stan's brother, Al, and six times Emmy nominated, three times winner, director Joe Sargent.

"What's up?" I asked.

"Got this call from my agent," Millard explained. "Scott Free Productions wants me for a screenplay. So I'll be out for a bit."

I blanched when I heard the considerable sum they were paying him.

"How'd you get it?"

"Well, they read an original script I recently finished that a director wants to make. And that book I came out with four years ago..."

A pretty traditional conversation between writers. Except for one factor. The man was eighty-six years old. Eighty-six! Since then all he's done is write a published novel, "*Bowl Of Cherries*" (McSweeney Books), sold another one awaiting printing, and is writing a third, at ninety two! This in a day when most of us of lesser decades find the industry's doors shut in our faces, decry ageism, claim we wouldn't accept an assignment if offered considering what's being offered today, yet privately pray for the phone to ring.

Maybe there's a personal credo to be found in that speech he wrote for Spencer Tracy playing John Macreedy in the 1955 MGM motion picture *Bad Day At Black Rock*, for which Millard won his second Academy nomination, a speech many of us fantasize making to the industry powers today.

MACREEDY   You know, I know what your trouble is, son. You'd like me to die quickly, wouldn't you; without wasting too much of your time; or quietly, so I won't embarrass you too much; or even thankfully, so your memory of the occasion won't be too un-pleasant.

Unpopular as it is for me to say, recognizing that to some older writers this is heresy, I think that's a cop out. Millard's proved it. If you're a writer you write. No matter your age. You don't need an assignment or permission to do it, which too many of us have come to rely on. You do it, which is what's been so inspiring and enervating about those lunches with Millard, hearing that he *does* it! No assurances, no guarantees. Without his example, listening to him, his energy, sharing, wit and wisdom, his courage to face the unknown, the blank page, I wouldn't have written this. Without his early encouragement I probably wouldn't have written at all.

With it all there's something else all of us share at these lunches. I was recently one of three on a writers' committee at the Guild. Business concluded, the other two, both in their late thirties, asked if I'd join them for lunch. Over sandwiches and salads, the two got into what was most in their lives.

"Turned my rewrite into Fox last week," said one. "Some college MBA fresh out of Yale I never heard of has *notes?*"

"Yeah," said the second. "Had a meeting on mine at Warners. It's a go if I get Meryl Streep? Meryl?"

"Funny," I said. "I have lunch with these older writers every Tuesday." I ran their illustrious names past the two, which caught their attention. "Our meeting always gets around to the same."

They leaned forward, awaiting the imparted wisdom.

"It's, 'Well, my doctor says . . . .'"

On March 14, 2009, Millard Kaufman died.

Epilogue

In the mid-1980s, if you drove down Sunset Boulevard to the sea, turned right on Pacific Coast Highway for about fifty yards, and your eyes were sharp enough, you might see a lone man swimming fifty yards off shore. His exercise done, he'd emerge from the surf, all six-foot seven of him, dry himself off, slip on sweat clothes and sandals, and climb the steps to the overpass crossing the highway. Dropping down to the opposite side, he'd turn left a few yards till he came to a long two-story stucco building topped by a cupola built in the 1920s.

A private club for Hollywood High Society in the 1930s, it also featured Thelma Todd's ground floor Sidewalk Café. The blond bombshell movie star of her time, Todd died a mysterious death in 1935, her body found slumped over the wheel of her convertible in the garage of her business partner, dead from carbon monoxide. Theories about her death abound; suicide, murder, a mob hit, the mystery still unsolved.

Reaching the building, the swimmer would buzz himself in, climb steps to the second floor, turn down the hallway, past a half-dozen people at work and enter his large unadorned office complex where he'd shower and change into usually a plain white shirt, casual trousers and shoes, ready to address the day as his secretary would enter.

"Father, you have six calls."

Home to Paulist Productions for the past forty years, Father Elwood Kaiser was it's founder, taking over and redoing the building in the early 1960s. Executive Producer of multiple daytime Emmy Award-winning shows for the inspirational series, *Insight*, as well as network and motion picture films, the Catholic priest, Bud, as we called him, further established the Humanitas Prize in 1974 "To encourage, stimulate and sustain the nation's screenwriters in their humanizing task, and to give them recognition they deserve." As time passed the Award was expanded to include television in its various forms as well. Its definition was refined, the Prize honoring "stories that affirm the human person, and probe the meaning of life, and enlighten the use of human freedom." Cash awards went to the winners.

It did not draw the national attention of an Oscar, Emmy or Golden Globe, but to those of us writers in the industry who were nominated or won, it was of special significance, because it defined what you were, something I'd been striving to determine for myself for nearly thirty years. In 1985 I was nominated, quest achieved. As a dividend it brought me in touch with Father Kaiser, the two of us becoming fast friends. We had lunches together, dinners together. He married my step son, Andy, and his wife, Theresa. He christened their baby, Amanda. There were discussions of theology, especially over my inability to understand God.

"Think the mystery," he'd tell me. "Think what you can't explain. Start there."

"I want you there when I go," I told him one day.

"I'll make a Catholic out of you yet," he said.

"No, you won't. But I want you there."

But before that conversation there was a call one May morning several years earlier.

"You free for dinner?"

"Sure."

"Pick me up. Let's go to Matteos."

Over dinner he told me what was on his mind. The annual Humanitas Awards Luncheon was to be held, as usual, later that summer. He wanted me to give the key address that year.

"You're kidding."

"I think you've got something to say."

"Like what?"

"What you told me once. About that trip to Egypt, and what happened after."

Bud had a way of putting you on the spot. Writers who wrote for him on *Insight* were forever induced to donate their pay back to the cause. How he got away with it was forever a topic of conversation among us. No one ever figured out how he did it. But he did. You just couldn't refuse him. Nor could I. Against all sense and judgment I agreed.

I'm not an acknowledged public speaker. Especially from a written speech, and this one had to be written. Further, Lorraine has always advised me, I have a bad habit of not looking up as I speak, but burying my nose in the text, which means the audience is forever staring at the top of my head. Also I have a tendency to rush my words. No need to. The audience wasn't going anywhere until the awards would be given out later. Schooled as best I could, I looked out over the hotel ballroom, at the nominees, producers, writers, studio and network heads, recalling that old wheeze about the fellow who jumped off the top of the Empire State Building.

As he passed the thirty-fourth floor he was heard to say, "So far, so good." I jumped in.

> It's hard to believe my journey to this podium started one spring day in Egypt, but that's what happened.
>
> I was with my wife, Lorraine, travelling with an American tour from Alexandria to Cairo, when a flat tire put us beside a canal. It was poor farm country. The water in that canal was rank, and women were washing their clothes and kitchen utensils in it. Yoked oxen were pumping it into the fields.
>
> When across the road we saw a dozen boys approaching. They were twelve to fourteen years old. They were carrying books. It was noon, and school was out for mid-day.
>
> "You inglis or you ruskie?" One of them asked.
>
> I looked at him. He was lanky, about five foot three, wide mouth, lots of teeth, filthy clothes. A couple of inches taller than the others, he was less shy, had straight-on eyes, and a strength you don't often see in anyone, especially that young.
>
> I was curious that he spoke some English, learned that they all, these Egyptian farm children, were learning two languages beside their own.
>
> Well, we just got into it. What the kinship was, I still don't know. But there was a hunger he seemed to have, a need to make connection with Lorraine and

me. Questions poured out of him, as though he was trying to crowd a whole relationship into the few minutes it took to change that flat, while his friends, less forward, timidly tested the waters with some of the others in our group.

As I listened it seemed the viral containers in his genes, five thousand years of a once glorious history, were in that boy, yearning for rebirth. You simply can't imagine his intensity, his need to emerge, to know and understand.

Across that same road suddenly a man came running. He was flailing his arms in the air, as though scattering crows. He must have had some authority because the boys backed away. They were scared. All but this one who was talking to lorraine and me. He never wavered. Nor stopped plying us with questions, wanting to know everything about us, about America that we were willing to tell him.

The petty official, which is what he seemed to have been, turned to him, shouted at him, telling him with a wave of his hand to get away from us. Still the boy did not acknowledge him. The official approached, jabbed three fingers hard into the boy's chest, accosted him verbally.

The boy's head turned, turned on its neck. A full head shorter, he stared up into the man's eyes. His own were angry, black with anger, with what seemed to be generations of rage against tyranny and control. And they seemed to say, "I am not afraid of anything. Not you, or any human, or anything." The official saw that look. It frightened him. He was twenty years, fifty pounds, six inches greater. He was of no mind to take this further. He lowered his fingers from the boy's chest, and went back to scattering the others.

As we returned to our seats on the bus, we saw the boy crowd up to our window. He gestured me to lower it, and on impulse, it seemed, he suddenly thrust his ball point pen into my hand. I was later to learn that this was a profound gift, that I should have given him my own in return.

For the rest of the trip that boy haunted me. In the army I'd seen two men shot. I'd watched two race riots, and been almost thrust into both. Nothing impacted me as much as that one moment by that Egyptian canal. Later I would understand why. But not yet.

When I returned home, I did what any writer worth his salt will do first, with parents and children and friends he hasn't seen for three weeks. I called my agent. I learned there was an assignment awaiting me if I was interested. A two-hour movie for television. It dealt with teenage drug abuse. Something about a drug center in Florida, basically run by kids who'd formerly been drug dependent, counselling kids who still were. I remember heaving a heavy sigh. It didn't sound terribly original, nothing much in the way of a new idea.

I was told there was a tape of the center's meetings and activities. Take a look. And I did. I said I'd like to think about it. But I wasn't enthusiastic. In fact, at that moment, I didn't want a thing to do with it. And it had nothing to do with originality or quality of the project. The auspices were the best. Marian Brayton's CBS Specials Department, and a marvelous new producer, Beth Polson. The idea truthfully scared the hell out of me.

I found out why pretty fast.

I'd been teaching writing to a graduate class at a university here in town, fifteen students who thought, based upon what they'd seen on television, it couldn't be very difficult to do. The only problem they were willing to acknowledge was that they didn't know what to write about.

I told them to write about themselves, that they were, as themselves, totally unique. That their view of the world and life in it was separate from anyone else's. Their own special view. And it didn't matter if that view would change with maturity. What it was today, to them, was what they should commit themselves to.

Most were very uncomfortable with that. Exposing themselves to public scrutiny was, as one of them put it, something they worked hard to escape. Most of them were much more comfortable undertaking stories they knew nothing about. Wars and executions.

But there was a sixteenth member of that class. And she saved the day for me.

She was not a student at the university. She was a woman, married, with near-grown children, a Eurasian, half Japanese, half English. Her husband, whom I knew, had come to me, asked me if she might audit the class. She had cancer, and was dying. He thought it would be good therapy for her.

The therapy, it turned out, was mine.

She was a beautiful woman, with a unique history. Born in England, her father, a Japanese diplomat, attached to his country's mission in London, was forcibly returned to Japan at the outbreak of war.

That was her background. And now, forty-three years later, she sat in that classroom, terribly shy, in fact sat wordlessly, class after class. When it was finally her turn to speak out, to tell the story she wanted to write, she said she'd been writing it, could she read it.

She knocked our socks off.

Her story was of a helpless English mother, well-meaning, but a child-woman, who was being raised by her twelve-year-old daughter, the father having been taken away. Though the mother worked, the child got her up in the morning, fed her, sent her on her way, fought with the butcher over the wartime price of meat, fought with the nuns at school over over-bearing authority. The welfare authorities finally come to the mother with an edict. Assume responsibility for the child or she'll be taken away. Which the mother tries to do, totally threatening the girl's accustomed position in life. Dilemma. Become a mother, lose the child. Do not become a mother, lose the child.

It was a wonderfully moving story. And it was her own life. In telling it, she exposed herself, totally, dug open old wounds, guilts, fears, angers. The class was profoundly taken. She had chanced standing up and saying, this is me, my love-contempt for my mother, this is who I was, and how I feel about it. Then and now, this is who I am. Just as that young Egyptian boy had done before that petty official beside that canal that day. This is who I am, and I am unafraid to reveal it. I will chance the circumstances, your bru-tality or your scorn. Which is why it so affected me. It is what I had *not* been doing, had been avoiding.

That night I called my agent and told him I wanted to write the story about the teenage drug center, which I did. Writing a story about a professional man who knew absolutely he could handle his own teenage child's drug abuse once he discovered it. In this he failed. Miserably. What followed was the madness, the insanity that ensued from his failure, the denial, the overbearing rage of impotence.

It was my own story. Painful to recall and tell. Humiliating in some ways because of my own failure to deal with and control my own teenage son's cocaine and god-knows-what-else addiction.

I wrote it inspired by what I'd seen two other people do.

You graciously awarded it a Humanitas nomination.

Frank Pierson once told you from this rostrum, "The writer who takes the chance to dig into his own soul is tackling stuff that is hard, not just because he is vulnerable, but because we tend to defend these areas ourselves, as private and secret."

I say it's the best we have to give the audience who will not easily accept this, but regard it as an invasion of their private domain. But if it's truth they'll hear it.

Credits

Awards

Christopher Award Winning Script
Edgar Allan Poe Award Nomination
2 Emmy Award Nominations
Humanitas Prize Nomination
2 Writers Guild of America Awards Winning Scripts
5 Writers Guild of America Awards Nominations
2 Writers Guild of America Service Awards
People's Choice Award
NAACP Award

Feature Films

Choir Boys, 1977, Lorimar
Posse, 1975, Paramount
Emperor Of The North Pole, 1973, Fox
Joy Ride, 1958, Allied Artists
20 Million Miles From Earth, 1957, Columbia
The King's Thief, 1955, MGM

Movies For Television

Baby Girl Scott, 1987, CBS

Prison For Children, 1987, CBS

The Girl Who Spelled Freedom, 1987, Disney-CBS

Not My Kid, 1985, CBS

Pope John Paul II, 1984, CBS 3-Hour Special

Peter And Paul, 1981, CBS 4-Hour Special

Scott Joplin, 1977, NBC

Escape From Bogen County, 1977, CBS

Mrs Sundance, 1974, ABC

A Cold Night's Death, 1973, ABC

Series Developed, Created Or Co-Created For Television

Equal Justice, 1990, ABC

Big Shamus, Little Shamus, 1979, CBS

Cimarron Strip, 1967, CBS

The Big Valley, 1965, ABC

The Lloyd Bridges Show, 1962, CBS

Target: The Corrupters, 1961, ABC

The DuPont Show with June Allyson, 1961, CBS

Writers Guild Of America Elected Offices

National Chairman, WGA, East and West, 1967-69

President, WGA West, 1965-67

President, Television Branch, WGA West, 1963-65

Vice-President, Television Branch, WGAW West, 1961-63

LaVergne, TN USA
07 July 2010
188617LV00010B/132/P